Energies of the Soul

The true story of a Spirit Medium

By
Kate Maesen

Second Edition 2022

The right of Kate Maesen to be identified as the author of the work has been asserted by her in accordance with the Copyright, Designs and Patents Act 1988. All rights reserved. This book is sold subject to the condition that no part of this book is to be reproduced, in any shape or form, or by way of trade, stored in a retrieval system or transmitted in any form or by any means, electronic, mechanical, photocopying, recording, be lent, re-sold, hired out or otherwise circulated in any form of binding or cover other than that in which it is published and without a similar condition, including this condition, being imposed on the subsequent purchaser, without prior permission of the copyright holder.

Cover design by Hilary Pitt
Cover photograph ©Robert C Auty

A CIP catalogue record for this book is available
from the British Library
ISBN 978-1-838359-47-8

Also available as an eBook

Dedication

To my children,
my family on earth and in the spirit world,
each sitter for their time given,
and all from the higher side of life
without whom the record of this work
would not have been possible.

Acknowledgements

My sincere gratitude goes to:
Adrian Horn for the editing, Ann Harrison for the original publication of *On Raven's Wing*, Dr. Mark for his proof reading and Greta Lilek for the USA extracts. Cover photograph with kind permission from Catherine Cousins

Contents

Dedication
Acknowledgements
Introduction 1

PART 1 ~ Behold the Veil 5
   Awakening 7
   Bubbling Spring 10
   The Steady Stream 14
   Apprenticeship 26
   River In Flow 33
   A Stilled Lake 51
   Team Building 71
   Living Science 79
   Teachers 84
   Sequaza 89

PART 2 ~ Comprehension 95
   Death and Transition 97
   Energy 105
   Unbroken Links 117
   Perspective 123

PART 3 ~ Spirit Speaks 129
   Child's Wisdom 131
   When Light Is Seen 141
   Growing The Soul 149
   Invitation To The Séance Room 165
   Conclusion 176

The journey of spiritual stirring,
awakening, unfolding and trust
is in the company of a most beautiful soul
Little Raven
His quiet dignity, humility, patience
and love without measure,
supported and sustained.
On his wing I am carried,
on his wing I remain.

*Little Raven (Hosa – Young Crow) – Peacemaker,
Chief of the Southern Arapaho*
– Inuna *–* Ina (our people) , *(c.1810–1889)*

INTRODUCTION

The choice to read this book lies within the readers' mind. The first few pages of any book are always of importance to lead you further in. In writing I am wishing to take you on my personal journey of discovery and acceptance and what is now the norm of acknowledging spirit, my own and those who have passed through transition (death) and are living just as they always have. By pushing through the stubborn door of ignorance and prejudice, I finally entered the séance room to work in partnership with guides and inspirer's – Little Raven and others from the most beauteous of lands – The Spirit Worlds.

It is a must that I start at the very beginning of my awakening into these unseen worlds and life of spirit when my lack of knowledge in this field was evident, and my mind and body was growing from child to adult. This journey slowly began unfolding into knowing, and later working with this precious gift of spirit energy. Energy with life, intelligence, personality, shape, movement, structure and with desires to prove a continuity of our lives and theirs. It is of discovery through stages, in a life with all the difficulties of ignorance, of an immature soul trying to grow in a very materialistic setting. Of understanding soul growth through exchanges of energy, communications, acceptance and pure love that few in the physical can comprehend. The complexities of working with advanced spirit beings. To understand and appreciate this brief period of life on earth, as opposed to life in the real worlds of spirit and where endless ascension, thought creations and progressive achievements, are made possible in environments created for the soul's continued existence.

Spirit informs that every human is predetermined to resume their life beyond the death phase, in accordance with the systemic course of natural law. The casting off the physical body is a natural occurrence allowing the soul's entry in the spirit worlds, which are separated from this earth world by faster rates of vibrations and lesser degrees of weight. The released spirit body transfers to the plane of spiritual consciousness for which the earth existence and experiences has prepared it. The purpose of earth-living is the advancement and growth of the individual soul and the capabilities it contains. This process is repeated and continues from earth to spirit, spirit to earth. With progression the spirit becomes perceptively attuned allowing more expression of senses and giving opportunities to enjoy all creations of beauty thriving in the spirit worlds.

Mediumship is not based on any belief system. It has been demonstrated through all ages to male and female, with or without religions. The truths it brings have been established after much questioning, examination, comparison and testing both inside and outside of laboratory settings. Spirit connections through mediums have been evident for centuries. It has affirmed that interaction with inhabitants of the spirit worlds is fact, scientifically proven and is amply recorded from biblical documentation to present day data. Those in the spirit world, when under appropriate conditions, are capable to communicate using varied methods, from thought transfer, mental intuitions, voice communication and visual materializations, depending on a medium's stage and ability at controlling spirit energy for this to be achieved. All in a desire to prove life – their life.

I sincerely hope by reading the following pages you gain and become a little more aware of the *Energies of the Soul*.

PART 1

Behold the Veil

AWAKENING

TIME TO BEGIN

The beginning of my spiritual education was likened to a spring, first bubbling up from the ground. It was clear yet sharp and cold, as my spiritual awakening had a combination of bereavement and bodily illness. On this journey of discovery, the spring turned into a stream, slow moving and hesitant at what I may find when opening this new spiritual door. On doing so, this soon turned into a fast-flowing river in the sheer excitement of finding and wanting to find more. In the gush for knowledge I missed many an opportunity to understand more, as this search and need of discovery came at the busiest time of my material life and I found it hard combining both.

The stage I'm in now is rather like a lake, the river flows in but stays awhile before flowing out once more. I like this stage. My material career is ended, life is at a slower pace, and I can now give more time to spiritual study and practices. I know that the river running out from the lake will one day gently carry me to the spiritual sea and home. Before taking this last, amazing and most important of journeys, the lake stage is giving much valued time and opportunity to prepare. On this last journey I will not need aeroplane tickets or luggage. The necessities are a mind packed fully with all the experiences I have been so blessed to gain and an unequivocal understanding of my destination.

Therefore, it must be done! It has been in my thoughts for such a long time and the time has come to strike the keyboard and watch the words in my mind appear on each blank page. This is no piece by piece autobiography, for that I'm not famous enough, and quite frankly there are few on this planet who know who or what I am. No, the reason behind formulating these words are of a different nature, just to be recorded and perhaps read and hopefully understood in time, rather like the hieroglyphics, a puzzle awaiting to be revealed, and for some perhaps, a worded passage in our spiritual education.

My wish, as an ordinary human being, is to recall and state happenings that have occurred so far along my life's spiritual journey. Materially life has thrown its usual ups and downs at varying times. I have had my share of hard and difficult episodes alternating in periods of ease, as the majority of human beings will have during our life's course. Through this my character was – and is still – being formed. There is no cut-off point, as while ever we are on this earth plane, experiences come and go and leave their imprints behind for all our benefit. As we mature in mind and body, these experiences ought to be welcomed, for through them is the key to the door of our spiritual growth. This is the real purpose of our earthly existence, an opportunity to touch the earth's vibration no matter for how long or how brief. Inside each embryo is a spirit awakening, a spirit that hears the call of progression and must comply. So far my spiritual teachings are keeping a-pace with what I can at this time understand. What I could not accept in my teens, I can fully accept, see and feel the logic of now. I therefore urge those seeking spiritual growth, not to dismiss outright what is not of your understanding at the time, but rather place the lesson, on a 'mind shelf' and bring it out at intervals throughout your life to gauge your own spiritual advancement. Growth of the spirit is individual, personal and no matter how large a group, movement or congregation etc., you may belong to, the onus is still personal. Each treads their own spiritual pathway and therefore is responsible for their own development. Help is there and always will be, just as teachers and principals are there to teach and guide us through our scholarly education. But no matter how much guidance we receive or how large the number of fellow students in our classroom, it is still down to each individual student to use their own abilities, their desires and inner strengths to utilise the teachings and achieve the results being sought.

Spiritual growth follows a similar pattern, the desire to learn and to progress comes from within, however, there are no governing bodies to say when your spiritual education begins or what your subject matter should be, and certainly no pressures 'to perform'.

If permitted I offer you an invitation to re-tread with me my spiritual journey so far, in the hope that my experiences will awaken your inner self and give you confidence to open your own spiritual door without fear or trepidation and to accept those in the spirit as you would yourself. To embrace and trust those who you have known and loved and will come to know more, as being natural as life itself.

BUBBLING SPRING

ADJUSTING

Before passing through the death stage into their true self (spirit), a relative or friend would visit us regularly and receive a warm and loving welcome when doing so. Why then is this practice reversed just because our loved ones are no longer in the physical form but have moved into their natural state of spirit? To lose the fear of meeting, greeting and loving those who are now in spirit, and for us to return to a more normal acceptance, we first require a conditioning of mind in order to take those steps, tentatively but rationally and set out our own course of action. For me this was my spring:

Bereavement hit my family and arrived when I was too young to feel any deep impact, with the passing of my two grandfathers' and paternal grandmother within a three-year period. I cannot recall any feelings of sorrow. However, aged ten, the passing of my mother's brother Billy in his early forties came with the usual shock and sorrow as it does in most families. Still events are hazy, and again I cannot recall the funeral or know how this loss affected individual family members. One evening my grandmother and mother were sitting by our kitchen fire talking, while I prepared for bed. As was our family custom 'reading a chapter' then saying prayers before turning out the light in readiness for sleep, was routine and I loved this quiet time with my books.

On this particular evening, a movement caught my eye and on looking up from the book I saw Uncle Billy. I still recall every detail of his features, from his glossy black hair to his lovely mischievous ice-blue eyes, thin, gaunt face and lob-sided smile, hands in pockets. He was wearing striped pyjamas and wrapped in a burgundy dressing gown with a braided cord round his waist, tied loosely. No screams, no calling for mum, in fact just pleasure at seeing him. He told me to lie down on the pillow and I remember feeling very sleepy. I awoke in the most amazing colourful place with uncle standing a little in front of me, beaming with happiness. I was distracted by the flowers and their shapes, size, colours, all of which I had not seen before. In our drab, grey colourless Yorkshire mining village, nothing like this was seen, not even in books. Our front garden consisted of a few beleaguered 'pinks', the odd daffodil and night-scented stocks. The back garden grew black and redcurrant bushes, a few vegetables and housed pets including, rabbits, tortoises, a tin bath with my brother's newts and tadpoles, all surrounded by an irregular privet hedge. When I visit the Garden Centres of today, I find no flowers akin to what I saw then, in that most beautiful of places.

Blooms cultivated now are similar but still look underdeveloped to what I was shown, and they have little of the vibrancy. The grass was emerald green, and I remember my bare feet on its surface, not cold or damp, but warm with a velvety touch. A large stretch of water was in front of my uncle, which dazzled and sparkled as though lights were playing on its surface giving off colours of a prism. I did not see the sun but remember a stunning turquoise-blue sky. On the opposite side of the water, on a grassy hill stood a large white building with many windows, pillars and open spaces. Again, at the age of ten, I cannot recall seeing such a place before and stared aghast at its size and beauty. Uncle Billy said he was "in there, getting better and was not dead." He said it was time for me to go. He then simply glided across the lake, so quickly and smoothly, I thought it was magic and tried to follow. "No lass, you can't come any further you have to go back." Back where? I so wanted to stay. But back I was in an instant; book still in hand and the bedside light still on. Murmuring voices of Mum and Gran were coming up the stairs, but no way was I going to tell of what had transpired, it was special, a secret for me to hug, plus even at that young age, common sense told me, who would believe such a thing? I have forgotten many things during the course of my existence, but this and other spiritual experiences have never dimmed. All are of crystal clarity, every detail can be recalled, no matter how long the passing of years. The showing of the spirit world is indelibly etched, cannot be erased, and sets it well apart from dreams or fantasies.

Looking back now on this, my first spirit contact, when speaking of it or thinking of it, I not only recall every detail, but I 'feel' the event deep within my being. Colour of the flowers, the feel of the grass the scent of the place, sweet and fresh. Also a child in a strange place, no matter how pretty, would want the comfort and reassurance of parents and home. But I wanted none of this I just wanted to stay. So much was the pull of this special place, it over- rode any sense of belonging to earth and earthly connections. As to why my uncle chose for me to make this his first contact, I can answer by saying that a child would accept the event readily and without fear, especially as it was a person known and much loved. A child sensitive to spirit vibrations, as I, would make a connection both easy and possible for a newly transitioned soul. My uncle Billy wanted to make his point, "I am not dead" and this he did. He also wanted to be the first to open my spirit door as he now understood the path that was being prepared for me.

The spring that bubbled up in me, awakened my spirit at an early age but life had to be lived and the experience and the events that my uncle brought were soon silenced by the commitments of earthly life. The spring was turning into a stream but did not commence its flow until my twenties.

THE STEADY STREAM

OBSERVING

I was unfortunate to lose three of my grandparents before the age of five, but my maternal Grandmother Mary was part of my life until the age of twenty-seven. Although she pictured largely, I really did not know her true character, she was just Gran and was there when needed. It was not until in the latter stages of her life and having had two cerebral haemorrhages, that she came to live with Mum, and I began to know the 'other side 'of Gran. Her illness took away her mobility and independence. Her world was divided between her bedroom and a fireside chair. She would gaze at what appeared to be a blank wall then turn and tell you things from your past, present, and more alarmingly for me – to come. For a while I thought this was related to her medication and raised concern with Mum but she said that Gran had always been "odd that way but whatever she says, just listen as she is always right".

The other strange thing was, the times when she was not staring at what she described as 'spirit friends', she sunk back into the illness of her stroke condition and at times forgot who we all were or gave endless requests for her tea and going to the post office for her state pension. In these days of my early twenties, I was half intrigued, yet a little afraid of Gran's contact with these then, unseen spirits. In my teens on outings to the coast, my friends and I would visit Gypsy fortune tellers who told us what we wanted to hear i.e. 'shall I get marry or be rich'. It was exciting, daring and fun. Gran was different and when things happened that she had predicted (later I learnt this was precognition), my interest sharpened. Sadly, however, I did not know this gift of Gran's for long. A window in my awareness had opened and was promptly shut when her final stroke took command.

It was a normal Sunday. My two children were playing in Mum's garden and she and I were preparing lunch. Gran sat in the front room by the fire as usual awaiting her meal. As I was busy placing Yorkshire puddings in the oven, I was literally knocked sideways, and thinking the kids had rushed in, turned to check their boisterousness, but no one was there. I looked at Mum and she was pointing to the doorway leading to the stairs, ashen faced she said rather slowly "a spirit nurse has just rushed through that door." I was shaky and she even more so, but we just got on with preparing dinner, in silence. I went to check on Gran and to pass her a magazine but stopped abruptly as her face and the right side of her body were pulled and slumped, her right hand clenched tight shut. Mum and I carried her upstairs and that was Gran's last journey on earth. For days Mum and I nursed her, and Gran never spoke or moved. Her eyes fixed in a stare. The Doctor said it would just be a matter of time and that no improvement would be given her by being hospitalised.

At the beginning of the fourth week I was giving Gran her usual morning wash, when while bending over her I could feel a tugging on my cardigan. Gran's right hand had unclenched and was holding on the edge of my sleeve. I froze and looked at her face, her eyes also moved, looked into my eyes and she said my name, not the shorten version, but my full name. I excitedly called Mum and said watch, I asked Gran to say my name again and she did and gave a beautiful smile. My name was her last word and she passed shortly afterwards. From the excitement of hearing her speaking and thinking she was not going to die, to the shock of her going was devastating. Gran had been there always, and I wanted her to remain. I also needed to ask her so much regarding her ability to see and speak with spirit, now hopes of this were dashed.

Sometime later I asked Mum, about my Gran's ability and how, even though I was close to Gran, I never knew her gift. Mum's reply was that she did not fully understand it, but it was all to be kept a secret as she could have gone to prison. This puzzled me more, how anyone could put my wonderful Gran in prison for what was an amazing gift was just beyond me. I felt the loss of Gran deeply and missed her so much. At times I could hear her call my name and decided that I must be coming unhinged.

My failed marriage, the loss of Gran, bringing up two children on a low income and the general struggles that life brings, must have affected my health and I became ill with swollen neck, face, rash and high temperature. Mum came to stay to look after the kids to which I was grateful and called the GP. He said he would make arrangements for me to be admitted to hospital and would call back. He never did, being elderly and overworked, he simply forgot. Mum being of the old school, said we must wait for the Doctor to arrange things, and while this did not happen, I worsened and felt dreadfully ill, not being able to eat and just taking the odd sip of water depleted me more. The night sweats were horrendous and weakening and reached a peak days later when I thought I had had enough and just wanted it all to end. During that night, drenched in sweat, I saw the brightness of a light at the bedroom window, it glowed, and I tried to work it out as perhaps someone in the garden was shining a light, but no, within seconds this light was in the bedroom and becoming brighter. It was disc-shaped, gold in colour and began to illuminate the walls, floor and bed in its intensity of shimmering gold. It pulsated and I was mesmerised. From it issued a cooling breeze, which was so welcome, and I just wanted to absorb this coolness more and more. I was intoxicated with a feeling of sheer bliss, peace and happiness, without apprehension or fear, but try as I might, I just could not keep awake when I so wanted to see and feel more. I slept until daybreak and on moving could feel the left side of my face was not swollen any more, I also felt much better.

Later in the morning through a neighbours visit, an ambulance was called, which led to admittance, a lumbar puncture with antibiotics and fluids, to treat, what I was told was a severe viral illness. My recovery was slow, but although grateful of the medical treatment, the real healing came from that Golden Orb and to this day, I still cannot fully explain its presence or indeed the controller.

Following my illness, life was pieced together with

parental duties, daily chores and the fitting in of part-time work. I thought often of the sequence of the Golden Orb and the whys and the possibilities of it happening again. So far it hasn't. Dotted in-between the ordinariness of life came, what was then alarming events. The feeling of someone sitting on the edge of my bed was a regular occurrence, hearing my name called and opening both back and front doors only to find no one there. One night I turned in bed to see a gentleman standing by the wardrobe complete with watch and chain across his waistcoat. I sat glued to this image, having picked up a tumbler of water plus my alarm clock to convince myself I was not dreaming and fully awake. The image slowly, very slowly faded. The time was **ten minutes to two**. The final straw came when, again while in bed, I heard what I thought, was my young son getting up on his, sometimes nightly, excursions down to the kitchen to feast on the contents of the fridge. I was about to protest when, in came a toddler, around two years of age. He wore only a nappy and sucked on a dummy which had a string attached with two knots in it. A mass of blonde curls and such large round eyes complete with chubby arms and legs. He took no notice of me and went to my dressing table looking at the photographs of my children. In normal conditions one would have greeted such a tot with joy and scooped him up for a hug and cuddle. I was petrified and could not move an inch. I stared fixated out of sheer fear. Now I cringe at saying this, for he was the most beautiful child, yet he frightened me, and why on earth was I seeing and hearing things of this nature?

The child turned, looked square in my face, and like

the gentleman before, faded, slowly. Although I could not see him, I felt he was still there for a long while and also the name 'Desmond its Desmond' I could hear clearly. No sleep was had that night.

When the kids had gone to school the following morning, I was at my Mum's home like a shot, asking her to please come with me to the Doctor's as I needed treatment, tablets, injections anything to make me 'normal' again. Don't worry she said, "You are like your Gran, can you remember before she died, she told you that you were blessed." Blessed!!! I took this to mean I was blessed with bad luck as everything had gone wrong in my life. "No," Mum said, "She meant you were blessed with spirit." No way, on no account do I want to be like Gran. As much as I loved that lady and was interested in her work, I was not going to speak to blank walls or have nightly visits from spirits.

I was disappointed in Mum not believing that I was in some way ill. Her solution was to go and see an old neighbour to discuss taking me to the Spiritualist Church. What on earth was that! I had heard of our own Catholic Church, Church of England, Methodist and Salvation Army. But a church where spirits floated about was not somewhere I would want to go. One did not argue with Mum, and she, I and our former neighbour set off for what they called the 'rapper's' or 'knock knock is there anyone there!' Mum and her friend were no sylph's and I felt like a slice of ham in-between two large bread cakes – still their ample frames helped stem my tremors. The said Church was a wooden hut, sparse, smelt of damp and freezing cold on that winter evening. I waited silently for the lights to go out and the ghosts to come, wondering 'what the heck am I doing here'. The lights were kept on, hymns sung – that we did not know – two ladies stood at the front on what was termed The Platform. One lady told me of things that had happened, and I was totally unconvinced as I was confident my Mum or her friend had phoned ahead and told them everything about me in order to convince me that I was indeed sane.

A second visit was arranged and was similar. This time a gentleman at the 'front' said my mediumistic abilities were beginning to awaken and I would soon work for spirit, no way thought I, and I was soon out of the door.

Weeks then months went by and still I saw and heard spirit. The little wooden hut beckoned again but this time I would outsmart Mum and her friend and tell no one of my going. It was the height of summer, and on opening the Church door, I was stunned at all the greenery and blooms inside. It was like walking into a garden of green, white, mauve and pink, such a riot of colour. I marvelled, what a transformation. I was one of the first to arrive. I quickly took a seat on the back row and buried my head in the hymn book, reading to try and stop the nervous shakes. Stretching out my arm to turn a page I felt a sharp needle-like pain in my elbow and noticed I was sitting beside a huge thistle plant. I thought how strange it was to decorate a church with something so lethal. It was tall and I followed its growth down to the floor to where I thought its plant pot should be. No pot, the thing was growing through the floorboards, I was intrigued. I started to look at the other plants and was opened mouthed as they too were coming up through the floorboards and also through the walls: bind weeds (convolvulaceae), burdocks and Rosebay Willow herb filled every space. The only carpet present was a strip down the centre of the Church forming the aisle and it too had suspicious lumps and bumps of no doubt more foliage trying to push through. The doors opened with a flourish and averted my attention as cries of "oh my goodness" came from a troupe of committee ladies. They demanded to know who was responsible for cutting down these weeds and why had this not been done?

There was no time to move any of the foliage apart from a bramble which lay across the front Platform. This was cut down with the bread knife and carried ceremoniously outside by three committee members.

The speaker arrived and I marvelled that he conducted the service through the bindweeds and rosebay without the mentioning of any. The first shock of this night was the thistle; the second shock was the message from the speaker. It came from my paternal Grandfather Henri saying sorry that he frightened me when he stood by the wardrobe door, and that the time was **10 minutes to two**. I was floored, no one but me knew this. The greatest puzzle was that Granddad who was such a devout Catholic that he attended mass every day, preparing the altar and ringing the bell that summoned the faithful, and was given the name of 'the old bell ringer', would not be seen alive or dead in a Spiritualist Church. I came home more confused than ever but comforted in the fact that what I was seeing and hearing of spirit was right, no matter how unbelievably bizarre, it was right. After much thought I decided that although this spiritualist place had convinced me of my sanity, their wooden hut and floral display, was not for me.

More months passed and I was on my way to town when roadworks stopped the bus for a good while. Looking out the window we were in front of a church, a Spiritualist Church! Oh thought I, this looks better, made of bricks and the style resembling a proper church. I read the notice board of times of services and decided to pay a visit. It also occurred to me that having lived in the area all my life, until now I never knew Spiritualist Churches existed. This church was much larger and as I had gained more confidence in attending, I thought I would go for the middle ground instead of sitting at the back. The middle portion of the Church on the left side was void of people so there I headed. A gentleman said, "Don't sit there, love", oh why I asked is it reserved; "no he said, it's haunted"! What really! His wife said, "Take no notice, he is only joking and come and sit here."

A whisper went round the church saying she's here, she's here, and indeed she was, for in came the President of the Church – Miss E Cliff. A little body with piercing dark eyes that flitted about, rather like a kestrel. She stopped in front of the empty seats and demanded why! A timid voice from the back informed her that the tarpaulin had come off the roof again and the forecast said rain. Oh crumbs, my heart sank. The invasion of weeds at one church, and half a roof missing at another, it was at this point that I started to appreciate my time as a Catholic attender, having been a drop out for years, when I did attend, there was no disturbance from root growth and tarpaulin was unheard of.

From this 'brick' well ventilated Church a message was given by the speaker a Mr Tony Jenkins, that I should form my own circle as there was strong potential for my working with spirit and they were waiting to begin, hence the nightly visits. I was given two male Indian guides, (unnamed) and a message from Gran – the truth of which knocked me for six in its correctness. After a few glances from the congregation I shrunk down in my seat trying to look invisible. On the bus home, I asked myself, what on earth were guides, (I had only heard of the Girl Guide movement) and what may I ask is a circle?

Mum was good enough to fill in these gaps in my spiritual education by telling me what she knew of Gran's time and work as a Spiritualist. I was nonplussed at this information, Gran a Spiritualist and Gran worked at the front of the church on that Platform! Oh my! What a revelation and where was I while she did this!! Mum said, "Can you remember her taking you to the old Co-op shop?"

"Yes," said I, "often."

"Well she and others met in a room upstairs to hold their church services and demonstrations." While I had sat clueless waiting downstairs in the shop, watching with interest and excitement as the Flying Fox money pulley system careered around the store transferring money from the tills to the offices on a higher floor. If lucky I was given a few broken biscuits in a brown paper bag.

My sister being a little older than I and so hoping she may know more of this information regarding our grandmother, I soon paid her a visit. She confirmed what Mum had said and I was even more stunned. "How long did you know?"

"Oh years" said she, "but we had to keep it under wraps, Catholicism and Spiritualism were worlds apart plus the Law at that time did not look kindly on such practices. I was about fifteen, and we went to what they called a Special, and Gran sat me at the front on a trestle pew while she began work. A lady introduced Gran, and in no time, she came onto the stage, sat in a chair and turned into a North American Indian. It was amazing but unnerving." This threw me completely – an Indian, what! The type with feathers, what on earth was an Indian doing in our pit village.

"Do you mean Gran dressed up as one?"

"No," said my sister. "there he appeared in full headdress as large as life." For me this was a step too far and I decided to put all thoughts of Gran and Red Indians to bed. However, as those who work with spirit know, those amazing folks in the higher side of life do not let you go easily, and questions without answers soon filled my thoughts once more.

Following my attendance at the two Spiritualist churches I began to feel awkward and frustrated at knowing nothing about how to work with spirit or the reasons why I should work for spirit. This latest information about my grandmother churned up my thoughts more. Over a period of time the fear of spirit and contact with them began to ebb away. Gran would never harm or frighten me. I saw her frequently and heard her voice. The love I had for her, came fully in as the separation by death was nullified. Wherever Gran was it was certainly not in the cemetery. I felt hungry for knowledge.

Although the Spiritualist Church gave the information that I initially sought and for which I will be forever grateful, I had no strong urge to belong or to attend meetings regularly. Perhaps the reason for this was that it had been difficult breaking away from the former Catholic faith, which I had known since birth. I did wrestle long with guilt but knew the break had to be done. I had and still have no wish or desire to belong to any religion. I had to be free to walk a path designed and steered by spirit – my own spirit and others from the spirit world.

This stream of thoughts and actions was not now sufficient for the ever-widening path. A river of knowledge was needed.

APPRENTICESHIP

TOOLS OF OUR TRADE

My quest for knowledge took me further from home. On enquiring and looking for spiritual meeting places I found Spiritual Centres holding regular assemblies, with visiting mediums demonstrating clairvoyance and clairaudience. I did not restrict myself to one Centre, as in my quest for more proof and truth of the afterlife, a wider search became important. However, with each attendance, criticism began to creep in at some of the mediumship being displayed. Although well meaning, some were awfully bad in their interpretation of messages and did little justice to spirit communication or proof, while a few, and I do *stress* a few, were outstanding, not only in their contact with spirit but exactness at delivering precise and correct information and also in their deliverance of philosophy. Attendance at such gatherings brought information, which began to be stored, digested and thought through. Confidence of spirit contact was deemed as natural to those attending. To my amazement, belief in this was widespread, not only locally, but nationwide and outside the UK. Where had I been for the past 30 years? – Locked away in a small world with one religion as the epicentre. I rather liked these meeting places, the atmosphere on entering being so different from the hushed silence of a church.

Warm welcomes were routine, and all services ended with tea, biscuits and a friendly chat, nothing formal yet still showing respect for the Divine and for those in spirit working in the light and energy coming from the one source.

Before one such visit to an event being held a few miles from home, my son announced that he would 'come along'. 'Oh gosh' I thought 'perhaps not,' thinking he would make a joke of things. Another thought told me, 'why not?' perhaps he is just curious and this may be his one and only time of attending. We arrived and sat waiting for proceedings to begin. The music that was playing softly suddenly boomed out and made everyone start. I said to my son "Gosh that chap should have known better than to do that, what if someone has a heart condition?" "What chap?", "The chap there by the stereo system, dressed as a clown, and why on earth is he dressed as a clown I wonder, but it takes all-sorts I guess?" My son's puzzled look rang alarm bells, "There is no clown there, Mum. In fact, there is no one there at all." "But there is, and he is messing about with the music system." As if to confirm my words, BOOM the music blared out once more and before anyone could reach the system to turn it down, the clown beat them to it. I stared at him, he was so solid, brightly dressed, painted face bearing a huge ruby-red lipped smile, a small hat with protruding flower trying to balance on a shock of orange hair, but I knew, like my son, no other person in that place could see him, not only that he marched straight up the aisle displaying boots of an enormous size, sat on a spare seat at the end of our row and waved a white gloved hand in my direction! – Oh crumbs!

The medium arrived late, due to traffic problems, and while trying to apologise, stuttered her words as she could see, what I had been seeing for the past ten minutes. "Oh my!" said she "there is a clown sat at the back of the hall and I thought it was someone in fancy dress but now I know he is a spirit." My son elbowed my ribs and whispered, "Blimey." The medium described the clown exactly and said, "He loves music." – 'Yes,' I thought 'and very loud!' I began to relax, knowing that yet again, there was nothing amiss with my brain or vision. This relaxed state did not last for long, as the medium said, "He has come to work with you, dear," pointing a finger at me "and he tells me that he is so pleased you can see him too."

To emphasise the message as being correct, she turned to my son and gave him a message from his uncle in spirit, which in my son's words, "It just blew me away!" Part of the message I knew, but part I did not, as it concerned the tragic passing of three young friends of his and again for my son, this information certainly hit home. For those like myself, on the mature side of life, you may know of a black and white movie of James Stewart's, called *Harvey*. In the film a six-foot white rabbit, which only he can see, attaches itself to him and havoc was caused. James Stewart had his 'Pooka', and I had a Clown! My son thought it was great! But I was uneasy. At many services 'guides' were given, Romans, Grecians, High-ranking Nobles, Kings, Queens, and I came away with a clown – Clarence the Clown!

My son's attendance that evening was with purpose. From a stranger he had to have proof of spirit for himself and proof of what I was seeing and hearing was right. This was accomplished in one go and secured his support in the work spirit had planned, then and to come. My initial disappointment at having a clown as guide was soon dispelled. Clarence or Clary as I prefer, turned my world upside down and brought laughter for many, and at times, chaos for me. He was good at 'appearing' – at times too good – and I soon banned him from the workplace and supermarkets but always welcomed him at home. As well as doing his job as 'funny man', his talent lay in clairaudience. Both he and Gran worked so well together and the two steered me through the early stages of working with spirit. Whether they worked in tandem or separately, the messages given from the higher side of life were clear and correct.

In the days of yore when Kings and Queens ruled our shores, the court jester was highly prized and praised. The gift of making people laugh is just that, a gift, and Clarence was a true professional and worthy of praise. In this my novice stage of development, these two spirit contacts and the messages given were relayed initially to friends and family members. Later as friends told their friends, then colleagues told colleagues, people would come to my home and 'a reading' would ensue. The reading took the form of cards. I was told during her earth life, Gran had a fondness for card reading and Clarence soon gave his input too. When Gran was working, my right hand would clench, when Clarence worked, the right hand went icy and sometimes white, denoting the whiteness of his glove and giving the indication of their presence and readiness to deliver messages.

Love of the historic led me to research the beginnings of divination and I was both surprised and pleased at its long history. Cartomancy, to give divination via playing cards its true title, has been present since the 15th century as documentation reveals gypsies in the New Forest adding them to their complement of fortune telling aids. 'Etteila' (the pseudonym of Jean Baptiste Jeune), and later, Mlle. Lenormand of Paris were the most celebrated card-diviners of the 18th and 19th centuries. Ettelia dedicated thirty years of his life to a profound study of the cards, earning him the title 'Papa of Cartomancy'. By the year 1804 Mlle. Lenormand's renown as an excellent 'reader' had spread and attracted Napoleon's generals, seeking advice and reassurance. Divination by means of the playing cards is little used today, so when the opportunity arises, I always promote this method. The reasons being are that the inquirer is generally nervous when seeking a reading – 'shall I hear something bad,' – 'will any past deeds be revealed or will a death be predicted.' All these thoughts make the seeker uneasy and tense. Each reading always began using Cartomancy – a familiar object such as a pack of playing cards cannot make a person afraid. Coupled with the explanation that a medium or sensitives objective is to help and reassure, the inquirer soon relaxes and helps them to enjoy the experience of spirit communication. If anyone feels that a 'common pack' of playing cards is unworthy to be used in this form of communication, they are sadly wrong. Evidence via the Cartomancy method has been given time after time, and brought those lost in the depths of bereavement, reassurance of their loved one's continued existence. A further reason for 'reading' with playing cards is, that unlike the Tarot, these cards have few images to prompt or guide. The medium therefore must have a direct link with spirit to bring through the all-important evidence. Not all have the opportunity, or courage, to be present at physical séances to achieve their proof of spirit, and readings with cards give most an opening for their first spirit contact. Closing the reading by using Tarot cards, gives the opportunity again to link with spirit and history. The origin of the Tarot is somewhat hazy but appears to be about the time of the Renaissance and much evidence is given that the Tarot has for hundreds of years been one of the most popular tools for divination. Going through many forms of depiction, yet Egyptian, Hindu and Babylonian symbols from the past can still be recognized within the Tarot, linking their original origins to the occult masters of the East.

Gran and Clarence opened wide my spiritual door giving me the first experience of, and reasons for, working with spirit. This being to aid those of the earth plane suffering loss of loved ones, fear of illness, reassurance when life's experiences hit hard, and for spirit to use the open link to convey their love and evidence of continued life. For me, this was a time for personal development; to experience spirit energy, albeit in a lesser degree than now; to trust in spirit and in what they presented; to become accustomed to their visits and acknowledge them in a customary way as I would any earthly visitor.

For many years I frequently conducted readings with cards, but as my development progressed, the readings became fewer. Clarence waved his goodbye and returned to what he called his usual employment of entertaining children newly arrived in the spirit world. Along with other entertainers, circus shows were acted out, to help the little ones settle into their new surroundings. His 'serious side' as he termed it, was to undertake more progression, as his time spent working clairaudiently in the earth's vibration had earned him an opportunity for spiritual progress. The loss of Clarence was severe, for I did not know then that this would only be temporary. My pathway with Gran took another route. Messages given in churches and centres slowly, stealthily, eased the transferring of one set of beliefs and dogma, into visible truth and fact. Working with clairvoyance and clairaudience with Gran and Clarence was the support and bridge needed before transferring to what is termed as 'working physically' with the higher side of life's inhabitants.

RIVER IN FLOW

UNFOLDING OF RAVEN'S WING

Life's chores, a house move, and career advancement came full on but still there was just enough time in my life to pursue spiritual matters. This came in the form of meeting and speaking to like-minded people, and the results were that we should form a Home Circle. My home proved the best place to accommodate our circle as at the time I lived in a roomy, bay windowed, three-storey terraced property. Through her work my daughter had moved away and had her own home, and my son was on the point of moving into his new home with his future wife. I and two dogs remained, which gave ample space to accommodate this important and exciting venture. The group consisted of eight ladies, all were eager and what we lacked in knowledge and experience we made up for in enthusiasm. I must go back to the knowledge part because, quite frankly, we had very little and were outright novices.

The Spiritualist movement had edged away from physical phenomena and its development and there was no one in our local area for us to seek advice or guidance from. Our first sittings were held in the dimly lit dining room, and our thoughts and energies were directed to one individual, who had been told through church messages, that she had the potential to be a physical medium. Not quite sure of the full meaning of this, however, we agreed to give it a try. We enjoyed our sittings, and at the end of each, those who had a certain level of clairvoyance/clairaudience gave what was seen or sensed during the session. Tea, biscuits and chatter ended our evenings, and all looked forward to the following week.

About two months into our meetings, at one memorable sitting, to everyone's notice, the room temperature suddenly plummeted to a chilling cold. I felt a strong breeze in the centre of the circle and looked up to see the outline of a spirit woman, complete with red headscarf and earrings. Before I could say a word, the figure moved towards our medium who saw the figure advancing, promptly shrieked, fell backwards off her chair and became wedged in the fireplace. I have, and perhaps always will have, a wicked sense of humour and the sight of our medium halfway up the chimney reduced me to giggles, and luckily for me, my laughter set everyone else off in fits of laughter, even the medium. The sight of her large white bare legs in the air and her ample frame spread over the hearth was something to behold and proved a struggle for us to get her upright. No doubt spirit took a sharp exit as no further work was done that evening.

The outcome of this for most of us, however, was great excitement rather than fear. Something had happened; we had had a result, but not quite knowing how or why. At tea and biscuit time, a discussion was held, and the consensus was that we should take things more seriously and make a greater effort, to gain more results. We must find books on the subject of physical mediumship but sadly our small library had none, and we were too nervous to even ask the librarian. We then turned to making a better place to hold our meetings, as one of the sitters had read somewhere that a dark room would be best, also a set time and day/night of the week. The solution was my attic. It had one velux-style window, was carpeted, and fitting a door at the bottom of the stairs would screen it off from the rest of the house. Once this was done and the window blacked out, it was perfect. Sadly, two of the circle ladies were not keen to sit in these conditions and their unease has always stuck with me. Our fear of the dark is inbuilt; it is natural and perhaps a remnant of our primeval days, when creatures of the night came out hunting and man was on the menu. Sitting in the dark is not for everyone but the majority of the group were enthusiastic. The six of us began a new chapter, and as before, our energies and thoughts were directed at the medium. The attic had pluses and minuses, hot in the summer and hard to heat in the winter, but still we soldiered on, and the months passed by.

During this time my material career took a turn, and I acquired a transfer to work a distance of eight miles from home. This transfer brought an increase in wage, which was something I could not dismiss. At our sittings I found it hard to keep awake and began to blame the travelling, extra work duties or perhaps I was anaemic. I had no concept that this condition was linked to spirit. Also, during this time our medium faced material difficulties and found it hard through her family business commitments, to attend weekly and her attendance became spasmodic. Still we carried on.

On sitting nights my health deteriorated markedly, not only was I now more tired, but my voice also began to croak and finally disappear, all through the sitting not a word could I utter. I also saw on a regular basis a North American Indian gentleman standing to my left and on occasions my Gran to my right. For weeks I kept this to myself, thinking why is Gran connected to Indians? I could also hear this Indian say repeatedly "birds of a feather", I have come to work. I finally told the sitters, who thought it was marvellous, I was mortified. While spirit was hitting a brick wall as far as working with me, I feel to this day, the next chain of events was coordinated by them. I was given an out-of-date Psychic Newspaper in a pile of other magazines and on reading it found books could be ordered through this paper – spirit books! I scanned down the columns listed and saw Harry Edward's book on spiritual healing. As a hospital worker and having experienced the appearance of the healing Golden Orb during my illness, I wanted to read how spirit healed the sick. The correct payment had to be sent and I had £3 spare, so looking down the column again, I saw *Visits from our Friends from the Other Side* by Tom Harrison. Both books arrived and I read the smaller Harrison one first, I read, and I re-read.

This chap Tom spoke the same language as me. He came from an ordinary Yorkshire family, as did I, yet with a difference, a Mum who worked with spirit. A weekly natural occurrence was theirs, like having friends round for tea, spirit came to visit them, they spoke, they moved but above all they were welcomed. Reading Tom's book put me at ease and any remnants of apprehension during our sittings, was soon gone.

Instead of worrying about my Friday night illness of tiredness and loss of voice, it dawned on me at long last that something of a spirit conditioning was happening in and around me. I began to accept the Indian gentleman and relaxed even more. The "birds of a feather" were repeated, and his name was given – Little Raven. Within a few days I knew his meaning of birds of a feather as my growing up with black hair, when most of the family were blondes, I was nicknamed Black Bird and so our names therefore were linked by both colour and birds. I told the sitters at our next meeting that this Indian's name was Little Raven, but he did not dress fully as an Indian and no feathers were seen. More months of sittings went by and our medium's progression as well as mine was on-going. Having linked with her main guide and been given his name (again a North American Indian) our medium wondered if she could find evidence of him at our library. As I was on annual leave I called in the library and looked for books on North American Indians. I scanned through many, not finding a name linked to our medium's guide. A large volume was on the top shelf, and I struggled to pull it out, and when I did so dropped it on the floor due to its sheer weight. It opened down the middle and there staring up at me was the face I had been seeing at our sittings for months.

His name was printed underneath this picture: Chief Little Raven, Chief of the Arapaho Nation date 1871. I found a seat to sit on. Not only was I stunned at his name, but this man was real, not something made up, not ghostly, but real and the written words about him, plus photograph, informed me so.

He was exactly how I described him to the sitters, no feathers and dressed in 'white man's clothes'. In situations like this I always go weak, and this was no time to change. I was weak through and through but the eyes looking back at me brought a lump to my throat and a wave of emotions on seeing him that is still hard to describe. It is rare that I'm quiet, I'm a chatter box, when not speaking I'm singing and have an abundance of energy, but over the next few weeks my stunned semi-silence continued, and I spent time thinking deeply on past events and wondering what would happen next.

What happened next was swift progression. The acceptance and connection with Little Raven was made, and the Friday feelings increased but now without alarm. Within minutes of my voice croaking and disappearing, my neck had a sensation of ballooning, the right side first, and after several months of séances, the left side, but not as pronounced. Sometimes I would look carefully in the mirror, looking hard to see what I had felt at the beginnings of our sittings, but nothing was evident. The phenomenon happened in the dark, and at that time, in the dark only. After three years of our attic sittings, a voice box connecting to my neck had been fashioned, mainly by the efforts and expertise of Little Raven. One of our sittings produced a sound, deep and guttural. It made the sitters jump and was rather like someone trying to say the first few letters of the alphabet. After these initial sounds, Raven's name was heard. At first the process was not easy for me, and the effort drained my energy. But a cup of tea and a good night's sleep soon restored my vitality.

Our sittings began to take a different course. Our

medium would begin the proceedings, channelling her guide and the second half of the sitting was given over to Raven, to practice with the voice box. Little Raven always came and still does come in, on my left side while Gran remains on my right, at times holding my hand, which folds into a claw-like shape, replicating her own hand through her stroke condition. She brings reassurance and the stability needed to adjust me back fully into the earth's vibration following séances. Trust between these two beautiful souls grew and soon words were formed, and sentences made. When I hear recordings of Little Raven's voice, from the early 1990's to the present date, there is no variation in tone or pitch, and he still delivers encouragement, compassion, knowledge and guidance to the sitters and myself. On occasion my Gran works through me with clairvoyance and clairaudience as do other guides and helpers, but Raven is and remains the main controller of the voice box and we are inextricably linked on a pathway of friendship, deep understanding and acceptance of each other and our joint progression.

My reading of Tom Harrison's account of his mother's mediumship (Minnie Harrison) came into play again. Tom not only wrote about their weekly sittings but toured the country giving talks. At a town nearby he came to give such a talk, together with a slide show of the phenomena produced at their séances. Our circle members were fortunate enough to acquire tickets and were spellbound as Tom took us back in time to a parlour in Middlesbrough where wondrous things transpired. At the end of his talk, Tom left a picture of the circle members showing on the projection screen, while he signed copies of his book.

The finances raised by Tom's books were donated to cancer patients. At the time our local hospital was raising funds for a mammogram and unit to accommodate the increasing number of breast cancer patients. Having lost a young work colleague to this dreaded disease, the rest of the office staff took part in events to help raise the much-needed funds. Tom requested anyone who needed monetary help with regard to cancer patients, to come up and speak to him. I was wondering if Tom would be kind enough to make a donation to our cause when the photo on the screen of his Mum nodded and gave a small wink. I sat bolt upright and said to my friends; did you see that picture move? No was the reply but again the picture moved. Before I knew it, I was on my feet explaining to Tom our fund-raising efforts, which I thought I did not do too well.

He took my address details and smiled. Within two weeks a letter arrived with a cheque enclosed. When our mammogram appeal had reached its target, some months later, I wrote to Tom with our grateful thanks and enclosed photographs of the grand opening of the Cancer Suite. As an afterthought I put in a P.S. asking, "Before each sitting did your Mum's voice stop working?" Back came a reply, no it did not, but I'm interested, please call, and enclosed his telephone number.

One call was all that was needed, and Tom became the encyclopaedia that I desired, for what was the crucial time in my development. He was there with answers, enthusiasm and support. He oozed the love for spirit, and this was infectious. In times of setbacks, lack of confidence and frustration, a few words from Tom, soon put things right. Mediumship at any level is seldom smooth and Tom understood this well. His presence at our séances and in turn our sittings in Tom's home were the sound platform I needed to trust spirit and to work with spirit more. From that point the partnership between Raven and myself was cemented and I would not, or could not, be living my earthly life without daily contact with him and those in the spirit world. They are my family; they are my teachers, and my all.

Life still threw in its ups and downs. Our medium could no longer attend the sittings through growing business and family needs. For material and lifestyle reasons, other sitters began to fade. Even Tom and his wife Ann moved to Spain. It was sad to see this breakdown, but at that stage in my spiritual development I did not comprehend that sometimes changes are vital in certain areas of mediumship and new energies in the form of sitters are needed, not only to enhance the work, but to advance it.

During this episode of loss of sitters, I too made plans not only of moving home and workplace but moving county, to join my daughter, and to where I still live today. Better prospects both in career and living standards were offered and gratefully taken. In spite of this huge upheaval, spirit found a way to hold on to what had been previously built. Once settled in home and career, a new circle was formed, and the work moved forward.

The year's spent sitting with 'the attic ladies' cannot be thanked lightly. All were part of that new and amazing venture, from the embryo to its fruition. Their patience, characters and dedication were the very essence of ingredients required to bring through those first spirit contacts. Their strength, and at times humour, helped me to adjust to the changes spirit needed to produce the energy, in order for Raven to build the voice box, for spirit to speak through. Their greatest contribution was unquestionably their belief in the spirit world and the communication given by spirit, each week. To the outside world, a group of ordinary working-class women, family members, mothers, sisters, aunts, wives.

But each Friday evening at a given time and place, all would lose these identities, put aside their earthly roles and become one with spirit, instruments for the spirit team to use, a collective force with one purpose. They gave without expectation or demands. Without monetary gain, egos or notoriety, just selfless time and effort were their gifts to spirit with love and with the determination to prove life after life. To attend week after week, took organisation of their lives and some even ran the risk of ridicule. From all an effort was needed to travel and arrive on time having rushed from material work, or family commitments. But week on week this was achieved and slowly the efforts were rewarded. We came together just to' try' and we parted in achieving, knowing spirit and ourselves better, but above all, knowing some of the wonders of life in the spirit world and the wonderful beings who inhabit. Ladies my gratitude is yours, you are often in my thoughts.

Forming a new circle took time, some stayed some left. My spiritual education continued. Sitting with, and for spirit, I found at times complex. It was not all about just 'sitting' to see what happens. Some sitters expected results in weeks. Some were there with the intention of becoming mediums themselves or the wish to earn money and fame. Some were afraid of the dark conditions and some just could not sit still for ten minutes without wanting to move around and stretch their legs. This was all new to me and I began to appreciate and miss the attic sitters and sessions. But this was, I now know, just another experience for Raven to teach and me to learn by, that right sitters mean the right work. Not all sitters are suited to the production of certain physical phenomena, whether this be their temperament or energy. That does not mean to say they will not have the right energies for other physical or spiritual work.

I went through a lengthy process of trying to find what I thought were the right people, but failed time on time. This caused stress, frustration and thoughts of 'is all this worth it'. Trying was my biggest error. For in trying I was not trusting and in not trusting I was not listening. Little Raven, as a good parent does, lets a child have a period of learning by themselves before gently stepping in when errors are made. I certainly made errors and in my depths of despair, Raven called. He, who had been instrumental in building the voice box and knowing fully its mechanism, would undoubtedly be the one to know what energies were needed to progress it further. When I finally gave in and let Raven take over, within a week a chance word to a work colleague regarding spirit matters, brought unexpected results, for within a month a circle of four was formed and just as in the attic days, lasted a number of years. The ease of which this happened still amazes me and trusting spirit although not easy for me through being too reliant on self, began to make sense. When I say trusting I do not mean, that we are flippant and should leave everything up to spirit. We must live our lives and make our own decisions regarding that life, but the trusting of spirit with the inner workings of spirit is, I now know, essential as they have the supreme knowledge and understanding of the energy and ingredients needed to produce phenomena, not just from themselves but the medium and the correct sitters.

My daughter, even in the attic days, when her work permitted, joined in our sittings and does so still. As her material work entails oversees travel, it is not easy to attend on a regular basis but her empty chair remains in situ and in times of her attendance, her energy is added to the mix. Throughout my development she, and on occasion my son, have attended séances, supported and kept me going, especially through the lean times, when sitters had melted away and were hard to replace. I have heard from many people how hard it is for them to express their belief in spirit openly and have through family pressure been unable to work for spirit. Such sadness this brings, but such joy do I have, in having the support of my children, without censure or ridicule.

I am so fortunate that I can work with spirit as naturally as I can work in my home or garden. There is no condemnation from either my daughter or son. They have had their proof of spirit and the life to come, and in doing so, have an unshakable belief in the presence and communications from life beyond our earth and frames.

Our new circle ran similar to the 'attic' ways and faced life's problems also, fitting it in with home life, careers, illness and holidays and so on. Like the attic nights, the dedication and love was there too, and grew. Each week brought progress and a variety of spirit characters were able to use the voice box and be recorded. After two years of sitting a small red light was introduced at intervals in order to see energy building around my face and upper body and for 'spirit eyes' and features to be seen.

Spirit accommodated as best they could with the conditions that were provided and gave encouragement without criticism, as during this period of sitting, I'm sure the room used was not ideal and certainly not practical. It was large, hard to blackout and incurred noise from both neighbours and traffic, but bless the spirit people as through all this, results were produced, and progression clearly given by being seen and heard.

Six years went by, and into the seventh life clicked her fingers and our sittings ground to a sudden halt. Two of the sitters emigrated within months of each other and one was crushed emotionally by family problems. I was knocked off balance and the 'old me' returned with "Oh gosh, surely this is the end?" Well I thought, my material career was nearing completion and retirement was imminent so as well as hanging up my keyboard, I will also hang up my spirit chair and look forward to gardening, travel and what other joys retirement will bring. This was me trying to put on a brave face while keenly missing the members of our group and the work achieved.

Like the attic ladies, my gratitude goes to this second group. Our time together benefited all and placed a large steppingstone on my spiritual pathway. We as a group and individually, became stronger in character, more resilient in the belief of the spirit world around us, and for all of us to be ever linked with those in the higher side of life who taught, helped and guided us on that widening road of discovery. To these sitters I say – our energies will be for ever entwined and my high esteem is eternally yours.

Another piece of small but significant education was given. I had always believed that the larger the number of sitters the stronger or better the work would be. Clearly here I was given proof that this was not so, two sitters were introduced via an acquaintance and they together with the occasional third, proved just as good as eight, providing energies compatible for the work being undertaken. As in material life, some personalities take rather than give, and with a smaller number of sitters, a taker of energy is soon detected and changes can and must be made. There is an area in working for spirit that demands to be impartial. The acceptance of sitters must not be based on friendship, family or favouritism. The objective is for spirit contact and spirit proof and the deliverance of this depends purely on what each sitter can give in the form of energies that are gathered, blended, and added to by spirit, for a purpose, the purpose of truth. Tolerating someone who is not productive, disruptive and does not enhance the work is a waste of valuable time and they must be released. Previously I had experienced this problem and admit shrank away from confronting the sitter and asking them to leave. It seemed harsh and cruel, and I fought against it as this was not, I thought, the way of working for spirit. My ignorance blinded me; I was not only holding back the work, but the sitter's progression too, when they could be better used elsewhere. This problem resolved itself quickly and the sitter replaced to everyone's satisfaction and progress.

My retirement came and brought new material beginnings. After careful thought I purchased a smaller home, in the same location, but one that would best suit my needs as I grow older. It would be more economical to manage on what was now a reduced but sufficient income. The advantages to this new place are tenfold. The setting is quiet and its construction all on one level. The garden offers me employment, enjoyment and peace. We have a 'spirit room' to work in and progression is once more moving forward. Our spirit room is small but when blacked out it is perfect and we feel that instead of one sitting in a separate cubicle, we are all sitting in a cabinet and therefore united in what is given and received.

This I hope has given the reader an introduction to how I became aware of life outside the normal concept of earth life. The object I hope, is to express the ordinariness of a working-class individual, who like anyone else, can, if desired, seek out proof of the spirit world and beyond and actively play a part in the discovery. Although initially I may have been thrust unceremoniously into spirit awareness, those in spirit who know me and work with me, knew with my temperament something drastic was needed to draw my attention to their presence. Also my sense of humour would and still does carry me through, from the early beginnings to the present-day happenings.

The river of spirit awareness, that rushed into my life suited my then lifestyle and energy and gave me the strength to carry me through the early stages of development and to cope with its differences. This schooling was nothing like my junior, senior, evening classes or higher education received on the material. I had no manual, no earthly tutor, and apart from the time of encouragement from Tom Harrison, was solely reliant on what was to many, an invisible teacher, Little Raven. Apart from the reading of Tom's book and a healing book, I purposely steered well clear of 'spiritual reads', always afraid of anything that was read, may, in some way lodge itself in my subconscious and be reproduced at séance. I stuck to my favourite authors of The Bronte's, Austin, Dickens and other classics.

It is only now after years of development and in the interlude of retirement that I have the urge to acquire materials relating to spirit work, past and present, as a means of theory to add to the practical side, of working with spirit. I have gained knowledge, and now know that the energy used when building the voice box, was not of ectoplasm, as used with past physical phenomena. When comparing the energy to that of bygone days, or to the few mediums producing ectoplasm today, I was at a loss to describe it. Not being thick or glutinous in consistency, yet energy there was, and results from it achieved. Also, during the time of its construction, I and the sitters did not show any interest in its fashioning. Our interest lay only in those who were speaking and what was being said. Recently I have read the works of Robin Foy's Scole Group and in doing so feel that the energy and matter building in our circle was and is, of a similar if not the same ilk, as was used at their experiments. It would also explain the attraction of beings not of the spirit world. Although not having had an earthly or spirit existence, they have life and mind, and through a lengthy period and process of adjustment, have developed the ability to communicate through the voice box.

On one of our group's many visits to Tom Harrison's home in Selby, Yorkshire to conduct a séance, we all had pleasure in welcoming the return of Clarence, not only on the voice box but with the building of his unmistakable clown's face. Tom's wife Ann was sitting on my right side and had the extra advantage of seeing Clarence's face build and become 'proud' of mine of a distance of one to two inches. This heralded many such visits and his time of learning in the spirit world had been in the art of making contact via the voice box and transfiguration. This merited a round of applause. It also revealed a soul's progression from 'mind' mediumship via clairaudience into the more difficult connections of physical mediumship. Showing us that progression even in the spirit world is not automatic but must be learnt and earned. Clarence's appearance at séance was always welcomed especially when we had invited guest's nights, when there was nervousness amongst those new to spirit or the darkness. Clarence's humour would soon disperse any apprehensions. He joked of his size 20 boots and of his size 19 feet fitting comfortably in them. His remarks would cause the intended laughter from those present and gave the dual purpose to relax and lift the vibrations, needed in obtaining a strong link with spirit. In the late 1990's Clarence again left our meetings, enrolling in yet another spirit course, which I'm sure is linked to the work now being undertaken. I'm confident he will not be left behind in anyway and will no doubt be planning his third return.

The above mentioned notes, that at this stage of development our group was confident to receive guests to our sittings and in turn visit other homes to conduct séances – it was and still is imperative (whether sittings are held at home or from the home) for the medium to be placed (if possible) in front of a solid wall, in order to dispel any thoughts of fraud being given of trap doors, concealed openings or human interference etc. The majority of guests coming to séances are seeking proof and on the onset of each sitting, the more at ease with the conditions presented the more they are likely to accept the work is of spirit and not trickery.

A STILLED LAKE

TRANQUIL

I have entered my lake. Life just ripples along now. Time is on my side, and I dictate its speed. There is no rush to catch transport to work or sit in traffic jams, no confined office space to be harassed in. No targets to be reached. No pressures, tension headaches or stress. Life is in a calm peaceful home. A garden to love and watch grow. Spirit friends to give welcome, to work with and time to know and understand more. With this freedom, I meditate, contemplate and recall. I offer another invitation, come take a stroll beside my lake, feel free to dip in a toe, while I tell you of the wonders of spirit, the experiences and teachings given thus far and hopefully much more to come.

As life presents uncertainties, especially loss through transition (death), thoughts then often lead to 'is there really life after death? If so where does this life live and how?' Hopefully the following may go a little towards answering these questions:

At a recent séance a sitter asked, "would we all fit into the spirit world as our earth's population was immense and ever growing?"

Our communicator (Little Raven) replied, "Begin to see your world as a dew drop on a leaf, this is the size of the earth plane, in comparison to the spirit worlds, and as these worlds are governed by mind, they too are ever growing. When your reasoning accepts this, also accept that beyond the spirit worlds greater dimensions lie. Do not see yourselves as the sole occupants of transition, for you are energy and all around you are energy. Energy is life and therefore connected to the source. All energy, in whatever form, eventually goes back to the source when the mind, state of light and purity is achieved. Experiences on this journey of understanding are many. Entering the spirit worlds and the realm you are drawn to, is but one open door."

The Spirit Worlds – I have used the plural for there are more than the one spirit world usually spoken of. As the locations are unseen by the human eye, it is hard for the seeker or underdeveloped spirit to accept or justify these worlds. An easy explanation is to view our world with rings surrounding it, like the planet we know as Saturn. In each ring lie worlds of consciousness. The energy fields closer to the earth plane allow spirit people the opportunity to connect and interact with the earth dwellers, sensitive enough to pick up their vibrations or energy thought processes. Science accepts thought transfers or telepathy from human to human but as yet not spirit to human. The mechanism is the same, mind to mind thought transfer whether in the body or in the spirit. Each energy ring around the earth plane are solid worlds to the spirit people residing in them. Having drawn the best qualities of the earth plane, these gravitate giving a tangible solid presence, whether this be life in all its forms of beings, flora, fauna etc. This flow of life force is enhanced by spirit minds and added to by their creative thoughts and actions, producing worlds of beauty, harmony and depending on the level of elevation – near perfection.

As our development deepens in spirit, then we can accept that other planets have the same systems of conscious growth and where lifeforms live out periods of development, not on the planet's surface but in the energy fields surrounding. Creative thoughts are applied in the rings and worlds are formed to suit all inhabitants, just as minds have and still are, creating the earth world that we know and see. The energies and substances of which the spirit worlds are composed are physical to those spirit beings inhabiting, just as our earth world is constructed to accommodate life in the body and its needs.

Gravity – Gravity is a force of attraction that pulls together all matter i.e. anything that can be physically touched. The more matter something has, the greater the force of its gravity. Large objects such as planets and stars have a greater gravitational pull. Gravity is the force that tries to pull two objects together, anything that has a mass has gravitational pull. The spirit worlds therefore too have their own gravitational pull. When loose of the physical body and the earth plane, we are pulled by gravity to the place compatible to our spirit body. As I have made the journey several times, I would like to attempt to describe the transfer or the 'pull' into a spirit plane. Some have described it as being tunnel-like or transferring there in an instant. The second explanation I feel may happen in a sleep or trance state, when little or nothing is remembered of the transfer. On occasions I experienced speed, seeing what appeared to be walls as I rushed past. On subsequent journeys I asked my guide, if possible, to slow the transferral down so I may note more of the conveying in order to recall and document. Small but interesting things I did note e.g. breathing continued, my vision intact and I blinked and moved as I normally would. I was aware of the whole of my body. In other words, I was still myself in every way except for a slight lighter feel of limbs, torso, head etc. I recorded coloured shapes on each side, top and bottom and can understand the term – 'like a tunnel'. The shapes reminded me of a mosaic or small gemstones in multiples of colour and lights. As the speed increased through the gravitational pull and the first level approached, the colours merged into streaks. The time in this state is very brief and soon the gravity attraction ends and the scene before transforms into a recognisable world. On this first level a newly emerged spirit is presented with scenes familiar to their life on earth, until acceptance and adjustment is completed. When I say familiarity, it is very much the same as our earth of desserts, forests, snow, oceans etc. When a soul has resided on the earth and reached its span of longevity, in areas such as the arctic tundra, that scene is presented in order to reassure, calm and give welcome. It is a feeling of home with friends and relatives giving their greetings and adding more reassurance to the newly arrived soul.

It is difficult to describe the unseen. However, we are aware of our senses and our innermost feelings, which connect directly to our spirit. The more sensitive we became in our development, the more we begin to feel. In the formation of the spirit worlds and their continuous evolution, one could compare it to being like an exotic bloom. On earth we see and have the joy in the vision of the flower and its aroma locally for a short time, whereas the spirit worlds encapsulate the bloom without its ever decaying, and what to us is an unseen fragrance, to spirit this permeates throughout their spheres, intensifying its scent. As its vibration increases, it gives intense colour, sound and perfumed pleasure to all inhabitants.

Personal transfer between locations and spheres – In the body, a coordinated effort brings about our gait – our way of walking. The brain sends out signals to the spinal cord, simultaneously a chain reaction to move the human body begins. Walking involves a coordinated effort of the feet, knees and hips. The human gait refers to locomotion achieved through the movement of human limbs. It is defined as bipedal, biphasic forward propulsion of centre of gravity of the human body in which there are alternate sinuous movements of different segments of the body with least expenditure of energy. Once this is learnt, mostly in childhood it is seldom remembered. The act of crawling, standing (unsteadily at first) then those first steps, celebrated by parents are perfected over time, stored in the brain and become programmed. The simple act of walking is far from simple. It is yet another marvel in creation.

In the spirit body, walking is still an option, especially to the newly arrived. However, the spirit worlds are vast, and walking, although easier in the spirit body, would not be a practicality in reaching far distant places. An interest to convey oneself between places, spheres or to visit others, are first engaged in the mind. Like walking, it takes practice. A desire to be somewhere stirs movement, a conscious effort to think about where you want to be, begins propulsion. When the thought process is mastered, transferring distances becomes a natural sequence with little effort of thought, just as walking and travelling did when on the earth. I expect this to sound as magical and fanciful, but we must cease to regard the earth as the normal for everything. It is just the normal for human life, not spirit living. The spirit body, its mechanism and worlds must not be totally compared with everything on earth. As the spirit body's composite is finer, lighter and is totally mind controlled, transportation is self-created, independent, and not reliant on wings, vehicles or limbs. If one wishes to travel, visit friends or other realms for pleasure, to educate or be educated, your mind's aspiration will transfer you instantly and in accord with the spirit world's normal, natural, custom.

Exploration of the spirit worlds are, as always, linked to progression, acceptance and knowledge, each offering an exciting adventure for the ever-developing soul and the expansion of mind.

Revealing of some spirit spheres – While being immersed in this slow-moving yet purposeful period of retirement, I can enter the layers of memories with all the clarity of vision and feelings presented at the time. Over the years of development spirit periodically showed themselves in their true form and gave me much needed and valued tuition. The first lesson came in the form of a monk, Andreas, standing serenely, steadily gazing and knowing that at his appearance, no fear or panic would arise.

As in the time of my Uncle Billy's visit, I was taken in an instant to a place certainly not of this world. However, unlike my uncle's abode, no pleasure or beauty was in this realm. Dense undulating fog was the scene presented. Grey, dank and cold, not unlike the winter smog in our cities of times gone by, the result of factory and domestic chimneys, traffic, and an uneducated disregard for clean air or its benefits. It swirled, crept and clung. It travelled round my feet, damp and sucking, resembling the vagueness of a swamp and bone-numbingly stark. No formation of trees, buildings or illumination, just gloom, silent and eerie.

The sight was unnerving and unpleasant; the feeling, menacing, desolate and of loss. The air stale, putrid, nauseous. I so wanted to be away. Forms appeared and shrank back into the condensed vapour, melting, dispersing, drifting, just drifting, without aim or purpose. One form produced its hand and arm, reaching out to which Andreas raised his cloak to shield us both. I asked why?

The reply, "There is a soul trying to steal light and the succour it brings. In this place light must be earned by change of intention. Former thoughts and actions accumulated on earth have created this place and have been added to by un-evolved souls over eons of time. The taking of life through the action of pre-planned murder, violation of others for self-gratification, the want of power and greed gained through destruction and devastation of others, demeaning souls in the human state by removing or denying their basic needs, these practices and more sink the soul and earn it its rightful place when in the spirit form."

No fires of hell were depicted. Here in this place was dread in entirety, the horror-stricken fear of who you may meet in that soup of depravity. The uncertainty of a stronger, more powerful presence awaiting you: a faceless ghoul to bring you further down into the chaos of undisciplined malevolent, diseased minds.

My lesson in this place of influence and corruption was graphic and sobering, yet in this seemingly hopelessness, progression was, and could be, gained. It was there for those regretting their deeds and wishing to amend, those acknowledging their wrong and desirous of understanding care and compassion. When thoughts from such are formulated, they are heard on the higher planes and the unselfish love of a fellow soul appears to gently and reassuringly guide them to an improved state. Retribution must still be dealt with, and acknowledgement of actions admitted, faced and corrected. But progression of that soul by an earnest desire to compensate has begun and all is never lost.

My return to the earth's vibration was again instant but the experience was lasting, without diminishing.

The next reveal was just as thought provoking. From a brief acknowledgement of Andreas' presence, a journey was made through a drowsed state, and we were met by a figure, expecting our arrival. Our host was male, in mid-thirties; his knee length garb of loose, white material gave an appearance of Grecian or Roman style, with a single gold cord at the waist. Bare foot, shoulder-length black hair, and may I say, handsome. His greeting of welcome was warm and friendly without awkwardness or strain. This took place in a temple-like structure, grey tiled floor, stone walls, pillars with open frontage, giving a panoramic view of what lay before. Our position was high and granted an overview of all taking place.

I'm finding inadequacy in expressing the vastness of the places visited and here was no exception. A metropolis, vibrant in colour and activity, teaming with life, the appearance Egyptian of old, in style of building, dress, flora, fauna and culture. There was leadership without slavery. The adoration of gods so far as I could see, was absent. Organization without chaos. A grouping of construction without need of reward, just pleasurable presentation to each other. A oneness to improve surroundings, and in doing so, improve themselves. The vision seen here was once duplicated on earth and vice versa. I felt happy here, there was so much to see, do and learn. I longed to walk through streets. Marvel closer at structures intact and those still under design, the true side of their majesties evident and so opposite to their ruined replicas on the earth plane. In this energetic thriving commune, space for all was there. The option to live close to neighbours or to have seclusion. Swathes of grassland, rivers, lakes, all with abundance of trees and blooms. What was common to the human eye while on earth was seen again here but magnified in beauty with the addition of more space and splendour.

I was beginning to acknowledge that when passing to spirit, a soul having lived a true and purposeful life migrates to an area in the spirit world where that soul is most comfortable. If transition brought an Egyptian to a place of snow and ice, the strangeness would bring instant fear and unsettlement. One therefore, is given familiarity and following a long period of adjustment in such a place, is then given licence to the discovery of new realms if desired or when progression is deserved. Discovery of new spheres brings knowledge and knowledge in turn, brings progression. A soul may choose to stay in their familiar place for eons of time or that which is our understanding of time, for there is no time in spirit, no clocks to govern and my stay as a visitor to these realms may have counted in minutes of earth time but lasted as long as the lesson was given and learnt.

Our companion expressed that higher more evolved spirit beings visit at regular intervals to teach and encourage evolvement and in one area of this vast place one such visit was taking place. He drew our attention to a procession of people; some carried baskets of fruit and others flower petals, all dressed in a variety of colourful wear for the gaiety of this visit and presentation. Winding their way some four or five deep to what appeared to be an arena of white marble grandeur. The appearance of this amphitheatre was stately and vast. As each took their place, their excitement was engulfing.

It was not my time or perhaps my privilege to hear

their speaker, I could only glimpse at the ensuing light coming into their midst and feel their wave of pleasure penetrate my core.

From the hustle and bustle to the serene calm of this realm, that I was so privileged to see, I was told that this is but of one portion in this dimension, one period of existence, experienced on earth, a thin sliver from a much larger domain.

It was time to leave – a last look at this spirit world and gratitude expressed to our young guide. A swift delivery back to earth living. As before all is remembered and will be remembered.

Before Andreas left, he said that such was his pleasure at visiting what he called the Colourful Realm or to me the Egyptian place, a further visit would be arranged. True to his word, one early evening while I sat by a warming fire, listening to the wind and driving winter rain, Andreas paid his visit and kept his promise. I was so accustomed to these 'outer' spirit journeys now that pleasure instantly welled up at the expected voyage. A drowsy state is the best description I can give. Weightiness comes over the body and a need to sink down into chair, sofa or bed, depending on my position. It feels half-sleep, half-faint. There is a gushing sound in my head, like water or wind blowing, pressure builds around the head then forward movement begins at speed, until arrival at the intended place. The transfer to each place is in the hands of Andreas. Expecting the same reception and place, I was bemused to find all was not the same. No greeting, no hustle and bustle of a thriving city, yet what was before us was engaging.

Vast displays of construction, some small, others huge, mostly in the style of a palace, temple or tetrahedron. All were wonderfully decorated. Many glistened in an unseen sun, painted figures and scenes of Egyptian life, familiar to those of the time, in colours of gold, blues, crimsons and more, the product of a skilled artist's palette. The style was certainly Egyptian, but what era, I cannot say. Amidst this beauty and skill of stone workers and designers all was silence and empty, a vacant vacuum as all was deserted. No eyes to see these creations or souls to live in splendour. I pondered at no occupancy and why something so wonderful as to give pleasure to all the senses could not be used and treasured. Before my thought was fully out, the solidness began to melt, like some mirage in a heat haze; stone on stone became ruin, not of time, but of man. Man in his quest to conquer, man in his thirst for power and greatness, mindless destructive man, strife in the name of his god or any other excuse that hides the real reason of greed and control. What did not bow before him was destroyed, defaced and left bare. This vision was once solid on earth, life in a place with all its features of living things, ended by man, yet recorded by, and for, spirit's education. I was witnessing a lesson, and just one of many to be had in the spirit world. If wished, learning can be from books, from teachers in the form of higher beings – or viewed. This was a viewing and a sad one too. A before-and-after feature, for anyone in spirit to see and learn by and for those responsible, an opportunity to regret and hopefully make amends. For us on the earth plane, watching this event on the small screen or in cinemas, we would not gain fully the gravity of such full-scale destruction and the senseless obliteration of wars, whether in past times or in our own time. Man is slow to learn that conflicts hold no victory. When wars strike on the earth-plane, humans often voice, where is God in all of this! Wars are totally man-made, brought about by immature souls, gravitating in low, negative energy and therefore far removed from the Supreme Being's untainted, towering level of existence. God creates, He does not destroy. Those instigating of wars are defacing part of His creative thought and must incur the consequences. Spirit inhabitants closer to the earth's environments are the ones involved in creating positive energy and healing energy to try and stabilise the disruptions of conflicts. However, so as man has incurred then so must man find solutions.

A sensation of being pulled backwards brought Andreas and I to the place first visited and into the feelings of warmth and united activity. We watched a while the joyous life and pleasure of living in beauty, harmony, – peace without oppression, fear, burden, greed or envy. The building of this place, not only of the structure but also of minds tuned into being part of one purpose, to share, to love to please to progress, are all achieved without the need for war, conflict or unnatural gain.

It is regrettable that we, when in the human state, are unable to emulate the norm of that which is in most of the spirit realms. As before, the feeling of being comfortable here, wishing to stay and be part of it, was overwhelming and hard to comprehend. Andreas said, "You will go to the earth's place of pyramids and feel the energy locked in there" (This I did in my sixtieth year.)

A two-year period followed, during which, through our weekly séances, development steadily continued. The use of the voice box became customary to our spirit friends. I came to know the presence of Andreas more, and like Little Raven, was comforted in the knowledge of protection and care. I was informed that he was the 'cradle to grave' guide; or rather a soul chosen that oversees your well-being and progress from birth on earth to re-birth in spirit. He had, and has, no involvement in the mechanism of the 'voice box' or other workings during our sittings. His role appears to be as guide and protector on leaving the earthly body into the astral, and as tutor on arrival. As the trust between us flourished, it brought with it acceptance and a further reveal and a lesson was shown.

A transfer to a place void of colour was made; I stood on the edge of what appeared to be planetary in nature. Rock formation could be detected and solid was the ground on which we stood. Stars overhead in millions, if not billions, dotted a deep blue canopy. Nothing was translucent here, the scale and vastness immense. Moving towards us was an illumined form. Human in look and male, aged with long straight white hair and gowned in a lengthy robe, tied at the waist. If earthly this figure would be passed unnoticed as the appearance was typically mankind. However, a difference was added. This personage glowed and gave off a surrounding light. The effect would have been lost in a brighter colourful place and I understood why the terrain was as so. The light was not dazzling or uncomfortable. It was pleasing, and when remembering this now, I smile;

such was the warmth of welcome coming from that being. On the occasions on earth when a full moon is seen, the intenseness of its brilliance dispenses the need for artificial light, such is the glow offered. The nearest expression I can use to describe this being's light and radiation was that of a full moon.

Unlike looking at our Sun, the light could be viewed and appreciated without dazzle. The beams ensuing were enveloping and its waves of intensity, filling. The smile of this being was more than a movement of lips; it expressed genuine love and pleasure at seeing and meeting with us. I was enchanted and wanted the experience to last and last. On turning he drew my attention to a far-off spectacle. It was what to me seemed to be a city in both size and construction. Like our companion it glowed and lit a vast area. It throbbed, pulsated with energy and life. Shapes could be seen of domes and high-rise structures, towers and elongated, lower shaped complexes. All adding to the light and movement both within, and expanding beyond, its parameters, rather like our own aurora borealis but more intense, silvery pearl essence in colour.

Our distance marred a clearer view so body forms could not be seen, nor could the exact nature of each building. As I repulsed the lower plane, here I drank it in and wanted more. The pull towards its light was magnetic and mesmerising. The urge to belong, overwhelming. The feelings of not wanting to leave my uncle's place was nothing in comparison to not wanting to depart this. I clenched my toes as the expected time to return drew near. On reaching and residing in this place, one did not return to the earth's vibration for any further lessons, development or experience. On evolving to this sphere, all trials and character shaping had been learnt and earthly progression ended. Yet even here progression would not cease, it was another rung in the soul's evolution. Our companion indicated our time here was ending. I really did not want to leave. Such was my reluctance, I moved slowly away backwards, step by step, still looking at him and the place of light-splendour beyond, for as long as was possible. In a normal earth setting, my not wanting to leave would sound totally selfish and irresponsible as my two children remained on earth. I can only speak of how I felt of the needing and wanting to be in this place, which did override emotional ties and obligations. It was not only what I saw but what my whole being felt.

On returning back to the earth's vibration I took days to adjust to my surroundings, duties and responsibilities. My head felt light and dazed, my mood heavy and I became restless, hoping I would soon return to the luminary land. It was not to be, but the memory is active and the knowing that places of such stimulating, exhilarating, all-powerful splendour and completeness are awaiting each soul's growth.

On recalling these and other spiritual journeys, things then overlooked are sharper in memory now. On entering each realm, I was there purely to view, retain and recall. There was no liberty to wander by waters, enter buildings or woodlands or speak to individuals residing there. I could feel the ground I was standing on and energies issuing from all that was before me, though perhaps in a diluted form. There appeared however, to be an invisible barrier that kept me in place, a connection still to the earth plane. Freedom to explore shelved and time for staying long periods, denied.

Analysing more of each spirit visit, I see in myself a pattern of progression. From being terrified on first seeing an entity in my early adult stage, to it becoming a common place event now. Astral journeying too becomes a natural, if not frequent occurrence. The stay in each realm visited, lasting a little longer.

Slotted in between the outer visits were more local ones and totally different from travelling with Andreas. Again I see here a forward step in progression. The first being alarmingly frightening and its outcome once again blamed on illness. The succeeding ones triggering what I describe as 'clutch and brake'. They caused tension through my body and 'hitting the brakes' or clenching my feet, was my defence at trying to stop it happening. Each outing began with again with a gushing sound, as though a gale were blowing in my ears, followed by a lunging motion of being thrust forward with the reverse happening on returning into the flesh. The sensations of leaving and returning centres more round the head, mainly in the crown area. Now after many such happenings, all is silent on leaving and returning, resistance is none as a desensitisation to the method, over many such events, is now perfected. It's a case of 'Whoops I'm out again'. Like the feelings noted when in the outer realms, I feel entirely without alteration, solid, not vapour, coherent not vague, alert and aware of myself and surroundings. When taking an exit, whether the rooms are semi-light or in darkness, my vision is crystal clear, in fact more clear than when in the body. With no restriction of movement, I glide from room to room, without falter or fear of harm. On first returning to myself and seeing my body lying in bed or on the settee, I felt freakish, now it's 'gosh do I really look like that or it is high time I got back in'! So far these 'outings' have been in and around my homes.

Over this lengthy span of working with and of being aware of spirit, I'm unable to recall any such dream to match forages around my home, into the spirit kingdoms or beyond. Also there is no newness in OBEs as these are well documented and taken seriously by some branches of science. Thousands of people of all ages have experienced them and been brave enough to reveal. I am only adding mine to the list. I have no knowledge of the cause or if 'local outings' are even linked to our spiritual progression.

There has been only one occasion to recall where an OBE resulted in seeing spirit and this may have been coincidental. This happened quite recently in terms of my development. During a hot sunny day, tired from long hours of gardening, I lay down to rest awhile. Within minutes I was 'out' and entering the kitchen. Stopping at the kitchen sink, I noticed that my arms were somewhat transparent, not as solid as they should be although they certainly felt so. Clear visibility of the kitchen units, floor and my feet were seen through my arms and hands. This did not cause repulsion, rather the opposite, and I became fascinated at being able to 'see' through flesh and bone. While looking around I saw that the cat's bowl had little food in and was on the point of filling it, but no I thought not, but better still, remember it as proof to myself that I had been 'actually out' again and had entered the kitchen. I headed back to the sofa and my body and sank into solid. Almost at once I could feel a pressure leaning on my lower left leg and sat up thinking it was the cat. The room was bright, bathed in summer afternoon light and visibility of the room and contents were clear.

In this shining sunlight sat a young female, resembling my daughter in age and certain features. She was certainly a relative, with large eyes common on Mother's side of the family. I called my daughter's name and asked how she had got in, knowing I had not unlocked the front door from the previous night. She smiled and I repeated my question adding, why are you here love? "Come to see you", was her reply. Being more fully aware now, this was not my daughter, her hair was longer and had more curl and in spite of the brightness of the room, she had her own brilliance and 'glowed'. Her dress was not the style of my daughters, being long, silky in texture and flowing. Tied at the waist by a dusty pink band, as opposed to jeans, trainers, t-shirt or top, the type of which my daughter would wear. She had her own exquisiteness, like porcelain in appearance and fineness. The only colour of prominence was her large pale blue eyes. She radiated ethereal grace. Another smile, a look into my face and the fading began. Slowly, effortless, spellbinding, yet when invisible, she remained, both in pressure on my leg and her very presence, intoxicating like the aroma of a rare bloom. I spoke, "I know you are still there, thank you so much for coming." On rising a short time later, I headed for the kitchen, to check the cat's bowl, yes, nearly empty just as I saw. The evidence assured of my being 'out'. Having lost a daughter through miscarriage, I have periodically been told from various sources that she had grown up 'in the spirit world'. Her passing to spirit being eighteen months after my daughter's birth, making them close in age and causing my mistake in thinking this was indeed her sibling. Previous sightings of spirit have not been so personal or as moving as at this meeting. The purity and delightful loveliness of this soul lingers and one which I treasure and hold.

TEAM BUILDING

COMPANIONSHIP

Most of what has been written thus far occurred in the early stages of my realization and the first processes of working with spirit. Once the voice box had entered its final stage of construction and tested over many months of practise by Little Raven, a steady flow of entities was introduced.

Their voices gave a marked variation of tone and depth. The first being an African female named Simone. On first hearing the voice we mistook it for male; such was the depth and strength. She spoke and sang in baritone key and had a hilarious sense of humour. Over many weeks it was revealed that this beautiful soul's purpose was to 'stretch' the ectoplasmic voice box. Week on week this was done and a weighty sensation was felt, not only around the throat area but also lower down on the chest. This 'stretching' was to accommodate low tones, mainly used by the male voices. Simone was always an awaited treat. Her infectious laughter vibrated through the floor, causing a ripple of merriment around the sitters. Her main complaint was her size and in trying to fit her ample frame into what she described as a 'bag of bones'. She did a remarkable job, and once completed, bade us a sad goodbye. Parting from our spirit helpers is never easy as in the loss of any friend. However, just as we leave working colleagues behind on the earth plane when moving on to pastures new, it often happens likewise in the spirit sphere. We do not own, we just accept their help and guidance, until their course of work is completed. For they too have a journey to make, and that journey involves their own development, whether this be in their own realms or migrating to others. Simone's work with Raven was commendable and her spiritual advancement truly earned.

Following Simone's connection came Lucy's. An Alice in Wonderland type image of a five-year-old. Though she always added a 'half' to her age. She was perpetually looking for her 'teeth' and while doing so brought laughter to the sittings and an intended heightened vibration to aid the work. At one sitting she at last found her 'teeth'! They were not lost at all, having grown in her mouth, much to her and everyone's delight, and making her voice reach even higher tones. Her singing of nursery rhymes, squeaks and high-pitched notes were evident and vital in stretching the voice box in order to accommodate the female voice and the higher octaves of a child's speech. The ability of this child and with her, at times a display of her adult mind, gave all a valued lesson. She spoke that, when entering the spirit world, speech if desirous is soon dispensed with and quickly replaced by thought. Communication is then open to all with no language barrier to stem the flow of tolerance, knowledge or friendship. However, when an earth communication is attempted by spirit through a physical mode, spirit must first refresh their knowledge of speech and try to match their voice pattern, as much as is possible, to the one used when in the body. No easy feat and although we expect much at each séance, I often give thought to the difficulties that must lie behind each connection, when trying to speak through an unnatural element such as a voice box, made artificially and attached to a being who is still in the physical body. Once all this is achieved and conquered, the communicator must then try to replicate his or her voice, overcome apprehensions and emotions and then formulate words to say. Sadly, many fail and revert to the communications offered by means of clairvoyance or clairaudience. Those that do master this form of communication give elation to the sitters and themselves. Lucy did sterling work, and like Simone, gave tireless dedication to their designated task.

Through her form as a cheeky, chatty child, her acceptance was instant and welcomed. Energies blended with Raven's and ours and brought a swift conclusion to tasks and purpose. Unlike Simone, Lucy visits often, and when doing so, brings the shy, quieter Desmond. The beautiful child who toddled into my bedroom all those years ago and who I once feared and is now a regular visitor both in and out of our circle. He has now adopted me as his earth Mum, and it is such a privilege.

More months of sitting at séance soon turned into years, I was given another test of trust. My usual reaction to anything new was always doubt and distrust and this was no exception. As each séance began, I often saw my trusty Raven standing stalwart and alone on my left side. However, one evening this all changed as another gentleman stood side by side with Raven. This spirit was totally different in look and dress, being fashioned in what one would call typical North American Indian attire. In other words, a full-length feathered headdress and white coloured robes reaching down to what appeared to be moccasins. He was slimmer and larger in stature than Raven. I kept this first vision private and did so for the coming weeks. He returned time and time again. Little Raven gave his name as being White Eagle and added another 'bird' to the flock. Sometime later I thought it best to mention the appearance to the sitters in case this new 'spirit' had anything to do with the present work or the work to come. One of the ladies' present was in raptures at this name, which meant nothing to me, saying 'he' was famous and spiritual teachings from him had been given and published. My heart sank, well said I, this chap cannot be the same one, he is just a pal of Raven's and so we will leave it at that. White Eagle soon began to use the voice box and gave a deep unmistakably male pronounced tone. For the next twenty plus years, through the highs and lows of my development, like Little Raven, White Eagle has been present at most sittings, rarely missing any. Over that time his voice has become stable and stronger and a little more fluent. Accepting Raven and my Gran after an initial struggle became easy and routine. White Eagle was never so. Because of the 'fame' connected with this name, I shrank from the connection, voluntary and involuntary. I'm ordinary, little known and private. I watch famous people on the TV and at the theatre, 'Celebrities' on any level do not enter my home.

The only way I could overcome his repeated presence was saying and believing that this 'White Eagle' is just not the same one who is widely known – he just has the same name and is a connection of Raven's. I'm sure this deep reluctance of my non-acceptance, stemmed the flow of what could have been many years of knowledge and personal progression. The loss is all mine and mine alone. However, White Eagle's patience of late has begun to show dividends.

As I've explained, I'm settling into a new home and surroundings. This was totally achieved under the guidance of White Eagle. He appeared one night by my bedroom door. His attire was unmistakable. The illumination from him such that I could clearly see the downy feathers of his headdress close to his forehead, moving in a soft light current. Above these snowy plumes came a magenta-coloured band before the full headdress displayed its magnificence of height and length. He said a move from this place of living would be swift, he would control its actions and I was to trust. He drew closer and I felt the sleep of spirit travel descend. I awoke at his side on top of high mountainous cliffs in a place of silence, twilight and breath-taking beauty. Sculptured crags, their tips bejewelled in crystalline diamanté, gave picture to an earth's hard frost. Each cluster set in its own light as though moonlit rays shone from beneath. Nowhere was static, foliage swayed in a breeze of energy as would life on a reef of coral. From high came cascades of pearl-coloured water, dramatic, awesome. Plunging at speed then lost in the darkness below. No thunderous roar to disturb the peace but a display of translucent, spark force. Amidst this glory, White Eagle stood, just as I saw him moments before on the earth plane, but so near now that I could see his dark eyes, the carved-like features of his brow, nose, cheeks and jawline. A half smile showing kindness, reassurance and wisdom. Oh such wisdom doth lie behind that still countenance.

White Eagle began to change, the form was still there, but features, attire, the solidness of frame where all replaced by stands of light, coloured lights of every shade and hue imaginable, akin to our stroboscopic lighting but interchanging at higher speed, in depth and brilliance of colour. This light display was of living matter and cannot be fully explained by my limited vocabulary. Each fibre had a myriad of colours that radiated from every part of his being. No sun was needed to enhance or reflect the brilliance as each strand gave its own intensity and direction. The strobes rippled and undulated as would a zephyr stirring a cornfield. This vision was mind-numbing, wondrous, and shatteringly spectacular.

I was lifted up, slowly, effortlessly. Arms held me safe and secure, there on the edge of nothingness when fear would be natural, I was held, wrapped in a coverlet of love and light and all my trust was given to the one holding me, the one named White Eagle. He said, "I will never let you fall" and I believe he never will.

This revealing lasted but moments, as I, in my human linked condition, was not attuned to engage in more. So intense was the energy, its strength, its beauty all in tune to this celestial place.

I awoke exactly as I had left, staring at the bedroom door, the image of White Eagle fading, fading and gone. Lasting and still alive are the feelings and imagery.

Two days passed and a phone call from the Estate Agent announced a couple wished to view my property.

They did so and the following day an offer of purchase was accepted. At that point I had no idea where I would live. That night brought another visit from White Eagle with the purpose of showing my new home. A bungalow, garage on the right, coloured stones under one window, red and green carpets, fairies and elves. The description of the bungalow etc. could be accepted but fairies and elves? A week later I viewed a bungalow, without thought of what White Eagle had said. I was so in rapture with this perfect little home.

The legal work was completed at speed, and I was quickly moved in. Over the next few months the things White Eagle had predicted began to register. Red and green carpets, coloured stones under one window and the garage situated on the right. When spring came and I began to clear the overgrown garden, there nestling in between shrubs and thick foliage were stone elves, and on clearing away ivy, revealed a porcelain plaque depicting the aforementioned fairies.

I must admit that I still do not know with any certainty that White Eagle is in any way connected to the White Eagle already in print. But I do know that this beautiful being is worthy of note, has earned the spiritual progression I was so privileged to be shown, and which in turn has given me the confidence to speak of and write his name in connection to mine. Because of my human failings of doubt and mistrust, White Eagle mastered that negative and gained my trust by showing his true self in spirit and in the realm in which he belongs. By giving such concrete proof in material matters, he left me in no doubt of his status and his kindness in waiting for me to develop sufficiently to accept him and his name. Now settled in this new abode, our séances are underway with weekly regularity. White Eagle being fully accepted. There is no hesitation in my thoughts only humbleness and pangs of guilt. He has become overseer of the new work taking place, which requires the transfer of stronger energy. This is in no way at Little Raven's expense, rather the opposite. When working in the séance room, Raven is the controller of me, of the voice box and the spirit people using it. I would always have reservations of any work being undertaken, without Little Raven's presence, such is my reliance. He is my best friend on the earth's vibration and my entrusted link to the spirit world.

It is not that I rank spirit in order of preference, but I am in the human form and therefore have human ways of thinking. I need the reliability of those taking part in our weekly experiments when linking with the spirit forms and energies. Whatever the experiment or whoever the spirit visitor, Little Raven and my Grandmother would never allow any dangerous act to invade or disrupt the work. Like two colossi they stand watchful, protecting, knowing they have the complete trust from all attending, especially mine, in or out of the séance room. White Eagle concentrates his knowledge on building and collating the now more powerful energies with the intent of producing spirit forms to be seen and giving the all-important proof of life beyond life. His purpose also is to show that progression is open to all.

Therefore, a team was formed, a family created joining two sides of the veil, a job to be done and the will there to undertake what is needed to reach the goals, being set before us.

LIVING SCIENCE

DISCIPLINE

Little Raven and White Eagle without doubt work closely together and have so far attended our séances in tandem. The security they bring to each communication time is immeasurable. The respect for each other's capabilities is often depicted in sincere sentiments. The encouragement they give to each sitter, invaluable. However, as with any course of work they are not alone. Materials, in the form of energies are required. These together with a good size spirit team are the essentials. Spirit energy is added in each sitting, and in turn, combined with earth's energies, the medium's and those of the sitters. The steady stream of resources is then refined, amalgamated, fashioned in design and texture to create an end product of all this activity, intended for the sole purpose of enlightenment or evidence of continued life with form and intelligence. It is also to bring awareness into our everyday mode of living, that life of the spirit is present, is constantly going on in and around us all, intertwining, loving, comforting, teaching, supporting, whether we acknowledge this fact or not.

Scientists in the spirit world perform such an importance in the gathering and distribution of these vital fuels assigned to spirit communications and I have no real concept of what their work entails other than that. Science, especially science of this nature, is far beyond my level of intelligence. But as a medium, a sensitive or receiver of this energy and their efforts, I can only add and relay the effects on the body and what occurs in the course of each union with spirit:

As Little Raven draws near, I feel varying degrees of temperatures. From waves of intense heat to coldness verging on freezing that at any other given time and place would, without doubt, cause the effects of hypothermia. I feel a lightness of the body, drowsy and the heart rate slows as an animal in hibernation. A current is felt running through my body with an outlet mainly at the throat, through the hands, the right one being the strongest point of outward flow. At times I feel a similar sensation through both feet. A swelling, inflating sensation is felt at the throat, followed by loss of voice or depletion in volume. The inflation spreads to both sides of the neck, ending below each earlobe. In this bag-like formation spirit are then at liberty to speak, with the flexibility of high or low tones, male or female. At this stage of development (2014) spirit informed me that as progression deepens, the stomach will have a similar directed force of energy, with expansion and flow coming through the lower spine and emanating out through the solar plexus. This energy will be denser in nature. The spirit-made voice box is not independent and is attached to and extends from and around the vocal cords. The spirit users have varying degrees of success depending on their own development and techniques. The head is the most sensitive area. Here, spirit hands or fingers are felt touching, also pressures occur, sometimes heavy, weighty. Downward flows of energy-streams emanate from the crown giving an impression of liquid on contact with the face and neck. It is cool and has the familiar electrical-current sensation. Sitters describe this sequence as a collection of mist, the collection point being in the upper body or lap area. The entry of spirit is through the back, the first point being at the back of my skull. Depending on the spirit's proficiency, this varies on how much or how little they can 'occupy' my frame. A feeling of 'pushing' through begins and a reproduction of themselves is then attempted, mainly in facial features, eyes, stature, size and shape of hands etc. I could not possibly explain with any credence how this manoeuvre is achieved. The controller (Little Raven) and the scientists have full knowledge and charge. I try to visualise the procedure of what is to me, my solid body, but is undoubtedly a non-jointed moving mass of energy, to spirit. A mass, which can be set aside in parts and replaced by the entity wishing to communicate.

When a good contact is made, I have often voiced that 'parts' of me seem to be missing, to have melted away. To try and make the event more normal I explain to inquirers that "the spirit communicators just unzip my back and climb in". To be able to express these observations is recent, in regards to the length of time working with spirit in the séance room. For the stage of development reached now is allowing me not to be in a deep sleep or comatose state, when the séance is underway. For most of the séance I am a little more present, yet the position is altered, and I drift in and out in an unperturbed condition with feelings of bliss. Hearing is acute but I find it difficult to keep my eyes open and I drift and float mentally in this, state, conscious of some happenings, yet in no way can I interfere or disrupt events taking place. All are out of my control and in the hands of spirit experts. At times during the experiments I can speak, this is limited and the strength of voice weak. Though strange at first, I now find the proceedings exciting and to be (in a small) part of the work, as opposed to my being totally detached. It is far more rewarding and strengthens my resolve and commitment in the continuance of working with spirit.

The showing of spirit energy and features are conducted in a red light, one of which we have been fortunate to obtain. The light made and designed by Mr Hylton Thompson (Northumberland UK), this ingenious piece of equipment is of no harm to the delicate energy, sitters or medium. Instead of the washing away effect given with a low wattage, standard red bulb, Mr Thompson has developed a means of lighting the séance room with a luminosity that enhances the work rather than detracts or disrupts the energy flow. The light sequences are used under the direction of White Eagle or the people of science and allows the sitters, at intervals, an opportunity to see progression and extends encouragement to the spirit technicians that their experiments and attempts at being seen are gaining success. Gratitude goes to Mr Thompson and his spirit helpers for this new and exciting addition to the work being undertaken in the séance room.

Therefore, work in the séance room should always be evolving; it is an important means of furthering the soul's progression. Giving licence and compliance to spirit experiments furthers our education on both sides of life. As our evolution is ongoing on this planet, perhaps faster than originally planned, spirit have also to adjust to the many waves of energy now used in our daily lives. Our world is of the immediate, no waiting time, no time given to mature, and all is required in a 'now' way of thinking and acting. These fluctuations in high and low energy levels require adjustments of the spirit teams engaged in communicating with the earth. It is right to express that mediumship cannot and should not be rushed. However, when it has reached the stage of the séance room then a view of experimentation should be adopted and a level of freedom given to those in spirit, controlling its sequence, that at each stage of progression, changes, trials, variations and practises should be accepted if applicable to both sides in order to give the spirit workers opportunities not only for the present earth's condition but of that to come.

I am mindful that not all spirit communications can be done through means of a séance room and not all have the desire to be so involved in connecting with spirit. But again I must emphasise that you are spirit and in our busy days that lie ahead, may we find a moment to pause and think of spirit in all forms, especially our own.

TEACHERS

LESSONS

I have been remiss in glossing over the acceptance of North American Indians and others, as easy. A somewhat lengthy procedure was undertaken by spirit in my own thought pattern before any acceptance on my part was fully made. Doubt on doubt flooded in. Messages given in Spiritualist Churches and Centres did little to convince. The first hearing, then my seeing spirit was dramatic and frightening but such as these initially were, it proved the only solution spirit had in attracting my attention and setting me on this mediumistic path. I did not prove to be an easy customer and the process was long and at times tedious. Perhaps coming from a Roman Catholic background helped little in my 'conversion'. I was set in my ways. The only education and religion I knew was through Catholicism. Like the first wearing of a new pair of shoes I found changing beliefs uncomfortable and somewhat painful, for in doing so, I had to begin to think for myself, decide for myself and search for myself, as opposed to having a belief system handed to me by others in classrooms or at a Sunday service. A new way of thought process had to be tried and learnt, connecting the mind with new ideas and viewing possibilities from both sides, instead of just the one. Over the years of being stationary, sitting in pews, hemmed in by others, listening to repeated sermons I already knew by heart, my mind had stagnated, and my being was robotic. The concept of something 'other' than what had been instilled since birth, was at first, difficult to comprehend. My Gran in spirit was the main breakthrough and by her help and regular presence, I soon found myself 'saying' things that would come true. Words would 'pop' into my head, resulting in a prediction that, in a very short time, came to be correct.

I heard Gran's voice, always in the right ear and glimpsed her often in my home. I slowly but firmly became mentally attuned to her and in doing so, forged a link with other people of the spirit world, themselves wishing to make contact with earth and with their connections. A line for communication was established, which gave proof of continuous existence and opened my own awareness more. Slowly, stealthily this eased the transferring of one set of beliefs and dogma, into truth and fact. Working clairvoyantly and clairaudiently with Gran was the encouragement and reassurance needed before transferring to what is termed as 'working physically' in the séance room. As is widely known, the dark conditions for the production of this type of phenomena are necessary but controversial, the controversy giving rise to working in a blackened room, causing suspicion and on occasion creating an environment for fraud, which has often proved detrimental to working this way. Sitting in a well-lit room, working with the faculties of clairvoyance or clairaudience I found was set well apart from working in this inky blackness. It is a conditioning that needs practise; firstly, to overcome, what is for most, an inbuilt primeval fear of the dark. Early man's fear of the darkness was justified and the mastery of fire to give light, no doubt welcomed. Adding spirits into the blackness of the séance, dictates a level of courage and complete faith even stronger than trust in order to sit patiently, awaiting their arrival. The séance sitter has and will always have my deep respect and admiration in committing themselves to this level of work. The vessel or medium is placed in a state of change by controlling spirit guides and their subsequent actions. The sitters, however, are fully conscious, exposed and sensitive to all occurrences and proceedings within the duration of the séance. Such bravery and such commitments are applauded. When first entering a darkened séance, I was not the medium and at first not totally at ease, but by the regularity and company of the other sitters, I became accustomed to the darkness at these weekly sittings.

It was also fortunate that progression was slow and gave valued time for adjustment and confidence in spirit to grow, in this light-excluded room. The introduction of North American Indians, Asian, African and indigenous spirit people as Guides or Teaches were dotted in with souls who had lived lives similar to our own but most from years gone by. They knew the techniques of connection, the safety needed before energy could flow and be transferred. The right conditions of a darkened room, necessary in keeping the energy stable and condensed, the importance of excluding sunlight, daylight and white artificial light, which would dilute and disperse their energies. The preparation and conditioning of the medium's body to accept varying degrees and strength of energies and chemical introductions, necessary to produce the phenomena, being attempted.

Acceptance of all these helpers was achieved but not without time and deep thought. Why were these spirit people drawn to an attic in a small, terraced house, when I naively expected spirit contact would just be with Gran or other family members? Thankfully, tuition from spirit, discussions with wiser minds and limited reading matter gave the answers. The emphasis placed on tuition from spirit and mainly Little Raven's. During earth life, the beliefs and lifestyle of North American Indians and those similar gave the perfect conditions for their spiritual growth. I cringe every time I read the white man's term of 'savages', for surely it was we who were the uncivilized. The belief and known contact with the afterlife, the interaction and reliance on Mother Nature, the communication skills both mental and physical with spirit ancestors, was their regular practice over many generations and cemented their right when in spirit to become spiritual Teachers. For who could steer us better on this pathway of progression.

We are told by spirit that the 5th plane of consciousness attracts minds immersed in the sciences, art, music, design and much more and for those wishing to continue in their creative and teaching mode, opportunities to do so are given to teach in the spirit worlds or through mediums on the earth plane, mainly in the thought transfer of words used in philosophy.

Those who are of ignorance as to what wonders have and can be had in the darkness of the séance room, I would say, before you decry this practice, first attend and feel the beauty of spiritual harmony, communication, selfless giving, tender love and respect. All this and more is created within the darkness. For those embarking on working in séance rooms I offer the advice of making the room as welcoming as possible. The conditions although dark to our eyes are not so to spirits. Your endeavour must be to reach the highest and brightest of spirit minds as possible. Remember these souls are coming from a pristine environment, no pollution, no untidiness or disorder only harmony, and above all love. Cleanliness of self and the space you are offering is uppermost in attracting the right vibrations of mind. Remember like attracts like so careful planning and preparation before and after séance will reward in drawing the brightest minds and the best of all energies willing to teach and guide.

When our first séance room was established, Little Raven kindly gave these words:

"Welcome to this Lodge – a haven of peace and calm, a place of reflection and progression, a tepee of communication with the spirit world and its people."

"STEP INTO THE DARK MY CHILDREN AND TOUCH THE LIGHT OF GOD"

SEQUAZA

INCREDIBLE CREATIONS

This next introduction deserves its own chapter. There is slowness when striking the keys and I am hesitant at finding the correct words to type when describing the unfolding of the next insert into our working spirit team. Development in the séance room continued, bringing not only knowledge but a stronger, denser feel to the energy. In this closely massed activity of matter came an energized form with voice totally different from what we term as a normal way of speech. Pushing its way through the ether, it began slowly, hesitant and gradual – like a gentle knock on a heavy oak door. It demonstrated difficulty at being heard, was metallic in timbre and formulating syllables and holding pitch appeared a monumental effort. During months of séance sittings, this voice, at intervals, made its entry and its effort. We became accustomed to its delivery and admired and encouraged the strenuous efforts of the life behind this strained voice. When mastery of the spirit-made voice box was finally achieved and sounds formed into intelligible words, a link was made from a source not of the spirit world. Little Raven, we were told, had the credit of 'teaching' this being to speak in a language other than thought and one to be understood by many. This new contact was the product of lengthy episodes of the coming together of itself, Raven and the spirit scientists to grapple with the difficulties of holding and managing this stronger energy. When achieved the introduction to the voice box and our circle's vibration, was attempted. At this stage we had no idea that the speaker was anything but spirit, a spirit with what appeared to be an odd sounding voice.

If told, I'm sure there would have been thoughts of aliens and such, and this would, perhaps, have led to great unease. Ignorance is not always bliss and stepping into this new phase of learning had to be done with caution. Throughout, Raven was and is an excellent teacher, understanding perfectly my thought patterns. He therefore presents each sequence, each subject, each newcomer, sympathetically and simplified, allowing confidence and understanding on both sides to grow. This new life source and I became well acquainted at a steady but firm pace, under the expert guidance of Raven.

Soon the new voice gave a name, SEQUAZA and we were told this is the closest wording that could be offered to replicate what to Sequaza, and his kind, are notes or waves of energy. Each being, when in their own sphere is known by light sequences and energy displays rather than the calling by name. Well briefed by Raven on the customs of minds in the human condition and our preference for identity, the voice understood SEQUAZA would be the name of recognition.

As the months passed, we added 'he' to his presence, again showing our humanness in male and female labels. As the voice was devoid of the feminine traits, to us, male was a preferred choice. Sequaza brought much into our mix of visitors. As always, humour in my life is never far away and he soon learnt the art of laughter and its importance to the vibrations. Sequaza is a regular visitor now and adds a marked variation to the other voices. Having never had an earth experience or heard the human voice, working the voice box mechanism in its use of speaking, proved a mammoth task to learn and perfect. On listening to these difficulties, our circle soon realised that there are no magic wands in the spirit world, and just as skills are taught and learnt in our environment, in spirit new practices and techniques are attempted, failed, repeated again and again before the desired outcome is successful. Until we are in that situation, we can only surmise at the process gone through in linking Sequaza's energy, through spirit's energy, through earth's energy and finally through the solid matter of flesh, in order to produce an effect. All in the hope of proving their presence and reassuring us that life of the spirit and its formation cannot be extinguished.

Sequaza is no alien in the sense of a sci-fi horror work. All energy is linked to the Divine source, yet all do not evolve by the custom of an earthly existence, which in turn leads to the emergence into the spirit worlds. Energy forms take varied routes of progression. Life in Sequaza's dimension is just one of many. In the narrow corridors of our minds and limited knowledge, we can only see life as is presented on this small planet. We know and will continue to know more of the universe within our range of telescopic equipment, high-frequency listening devices and explorations. But the life forms in the dimensions in and around our planet are yet to be fully explored and more importantly, accepted. Within one or more of these realms reside Sequaza's and his kind. Living, functioning, progressing, evolving just as we – and reaching out eager for contact and recognition.

At this time of our evolvement this contact can only be achieved by mind. Perhaps a day will come when mechanical instruments will be invented to be as finely tuned and as sensitive as the mind, and a door made possible to open into the life beyond our planet.

From time-to-time Sequaza has made the transition from the voice box, into the strangeness of the material of flesh with varying levels of success. The manipulation of the voice box took time and this new manoeuvre of controlling his energy to the point of mergence was even longer resulting in an ague-type reaction with me and perhaps Sequaza too. On withdrawing his energy, my body went into shock with tremors and involuntary jerks. I felt as though I was dropping from a great height and the landing not smooth. My head spun, I felt nauseated, cold, disoriented and drained. Why tolerate such feelings one may ask, indeed, but why not? There is no bravery here, just a dogged determination to be one part of an experiment. One phial in a laboratory row, ready to be filled with substances leading to perhaps, greater awareness. To feel the growth of knowledge between forms of life, different, yet in some way, linked to my own, overcomes any small amount of discomfort. Nothing ventured as they say, then nothing gained, and a little unpleasantness of the body is nothing in comparison to the weekly wonders received. One cannot stop just because a small measure of disruption is felt. Experience had already taught me any discommode would soon abate and the outcomes beneficial to progression, with progression being the ultimate goal. Today Sequaza speaks well with his conquering of the voice box. His strong energy, heightened vibration and my limited capacity to accommodate this, allows him to occupy the upper part of my body only when speaking, as he says, this is of no inconvenience as "legs are not required when speaking".

At a recent sitting, Sequaza informed those present that as we record each weekly session, so in a similar way, it is recorded by those in the spirit world and beyond. The purpose being, if anyone residing in these planes wishes to view the workings of a séance room from the technicalities of the spirit people, or the functions of the human contribution, they are then at liberty to do so. It may also be of interest that all events happening on the earth plane are preserved. The earth's history of evolving is imprinted in the universal mind and cannot be erased or forgotten. And as is the recording of events in the séance room, the purpose is also of learning for the advancement of mind. Each recorded event is there to be viewed when those in the spirit world or beyond are ready to move forward in their individual progression to learn from achievements credited to earth's inhabitants or the failures through wars and destruction. Just as we open history books and record past historical events, in order to advance our knowledge, The Halls of Learning in the spirit world hold all of life's history, the present and to come.

Over the years we have gained much from Sequaza's connection not only in the feel and strength of the energy 'he' brings but snippets of information. He told us that colour is of great importance in the workings of his sphere, and he often speaks of the colour we call blue, indeed blue carries more energy than red and in the séance room during the red-light sequences, the bringing in of Sequaza's stronger blue energy greatly enhances the work, adding to the visibility of spirit forms and their movements. The energy introduced by Sequaza is power and not blue light and therefore offers no harm to those present.

The use and contact with stones, in what we regard as gems stones, in both colour and the properties within each gem, are used as energy sources in his sphere. He was amused that humankind puts monetary value on gems and metals as these are gifts of the planet, in our case (Mother Earth), and is free to all when the real value is released (energy) and the wonderful usages are obtained. He once said that instead of viewing planets as uninhabited, view the energy surrounding each planet, for life is within the layers and in the waves of gravity attracted by each planet. With instruments you are searching for life beyond your planet and seeing and finding nothing, when the search for life must first begin within the mind.

PART 2

Comprehension

DEATH and TRANSITION

Why is it most of us cannot see the process of death, or what is more preferable to be called "transition"? It is because our physical senses compared to our spirit senses, are somewhat opaque. For example, we have air all around us but as our retinas are evolved and sensitive to light wavelengths passing through them unobstructed, enabling us to have vision, we therefore cannot see the transparency of air, yet we know it is there and we cannot exist without it.

Sensitive is the key word here. Our five senses are connected to the body functions, but our aim should be to try and elevate self in the knowledge of the spiritual nature of who we are. To have a deeper awareness of what is sensed rather than what is seen, heard, touched, smelt or tasted. We therefore must cover the topic of death in order to try and understand the life that follows this course.

The complexities of why the human lifespan for a spirit, through earthly birth, can be for some so very brief, is not for me to answer, for it is down to each individual the length of progression that soul requires in each sphere. The experience of an earthly body may be just for themselves solely, whether this be of length or short-term, and likewise their earth period may perhaps be a lesson or experience given to others. I much prefer to leave such in-depth questioning to higher and more evolved individuals rather than philosophise. My spiritual education, although deepening, is very much on-going. I have, as yet, so much more to learn. However, what I do know is the death of an individual often changes the thought patterns of those remaining behind on earth and many questions arise. Grief is one of the strongest emotions we experience. Decades of ritual, more-so in the western world, of how we treat 'death' have built up to such an extent as to thicken and make denser the barrier between ourselves and the spirit world, so that it must be extremely hard for most of our loved ones to cut through this screen and present themselves in their true self (spirit). This together with the reception they may receive of – 'I've seen a ghost!' – would be enough to put anyone off coming back, to visit us.

The whole concept we have created around death, therefore, ought to be unpicked and rethought. Much could be learnt from indigenous peoples such as Australian aboriginal cultures. Passed orally from generation to generation their belief in Dreamtime or The Dreaming, links them closely to the spirit world, giving a deep understanding of spirit and methods of contact. Death then becomes joyous and so it should be. It is the great releaser from physical containment, the giver of freedom to the soul. Expansion, knowledge, beauty and perfection are all to be had, following transition.

Our deep urge to live is, of course, warranted and gives each one the impetus to hold on to life and its precious experiences, but other than trauma or brutality which snatches away life in the cruellest way, the natural release of the spirit should be accepted as a normal process, as is the spirit's birth to the earth plane. Our rebirth into spirit is welcomed, prepared for, and eagerly awaited by those who are kin to us and those who have taught and guided us. On the earth plane those who remain, will miss the physical presence of loved ones or friends for a while, but this process, should be of no greater intensity than if that soul had gone away to university, gone away to enhance and further their spiritual education. A soul's passing should not be resented, or any blame apportioned to them at leaving us behind, as the passing soul is as close to us as ever and a thought of them can bring them closer. The maze of feelings that bereavement brings are not easy to understand or control, especially for parents when a child leaves, but if our changed thoughts could ease the pain – if only for a day – then it must be worth the effort of thinking differently from that which religion, culture and ritual have bestowed on us through countless generations of ignorance. We treat death in a whisper, voices are always hushed, – She's passed away you know—Hush, don't speak ill of the dead, they will hear you. Of course they will, they have not changed and probably are having a good laugh at what is being said.

Our change towards death and the awaiting spirit world will also be of more help to those passed or in a state of passing if our education of the procedure were instilled, instead of avoided. We have got things so right at a much-awaited birth. The medical teams, the parents having attended classes, read books, the purchase of baby clothes and equipment, all are geared to make this arrival as smooth and joyous as possible. Yet death – the very word is something we shrink from – is something that will happen to someone else, not to me, something that old people face! The medical profession is taught to save lives yet very few are taught to face death, as this comes as a failure to their doctrine. For most of us at our time of passing, the medical professionals are usually the last hands to touch us. Their educational care and skill should be more of a state of awareness that the passing of the soul has begun; it is being released from its temporary earthly body. A birth into spirit is taking place and is as natural as breathing, and no failure should be felt in not keeping that life on the Earth.

The state of mind for a newly emerged spirit is of great importance to that soul's comfort and its initial welcome back into the spirit world. The unprepared soul takes longer to 'settle' into his or her new surroundings, many being convinced they are not dead and are frustrated in being unable to speak to or be seen by loved ones still in the physical. The peace, joy and liberty to progress are stunted through ignorant beliefs and practices still held on the earth plane, such as shunning all thoughts of death and what lies beyond. For most, the mention of death brings an uncomfortable feeling, but if we do not speak of death then we cannot address spirit; for life through death is all-conquering, all-giving, all-evolving, and places the spirit in its true state and environment. The separation at death is the beginning of spirit life, and that life lives and is given the means of reunion – not only with those they meet in the spirit world but continued connection with those still remaining on the earth plane. It would make life and death easier for both sides of the energy veil if acceptance of transition and its process were widely known and taught.

Man is the highest type of being that has, as yet lived on the earth plane. We are self-thinking, self-conscious beings, and should, and must take, full responsibility for our earthly body, the temple of our soul. We are made up of a physical body, a spiritual body and an innermost body or soul. As for most during earth's journey, little thought or action is given to the innermost part of the body. The outer physical body takes precedence and the spirit within, is greatly overlooked. The growth and nurture of the spirit and innermost body is intertwined with the earth body's actions and experiences. The earth body brings the spirit body into contact with the physical world for knowledge, skill and understanding of the world through the many changes of evolution. When these experiences are ending and the physical life is expiring, and no longer of use in development, transition occurs. The separation of physical and spirit, allowing the spirit form its freedom of earthly ties.

The ideal preference to make for your own or a loved one's transition is at home in familiar surroundings. I know this is not always a possibility and the majority of transitions are taken in hospital or hospice settings. However, if given the choice, choose home. The reasons are control. You are at liberty to make comfortable the environment, perfume the room, add soothing music of your choice and soft lighting, the latter being extremely important. Remember a spirit is being released into the welcoming arms of spirit love ones. Those who have come to collect the newly emerged spirit need the right conditions too in order to carry out their task and duties, which are far better, controlled in the right atmosphere of hospitality, calm and love. Emotions are strong on both sides of the pending departure, to the sadness of letting go and to the excitement of those reuniting and escorting the loved one home. On the spirit side of life there is great joy and on the earth side of life sorrow. The loss, however, has no permanency and one must have consolation that the very best was done in caring for the well-being of the individual through their last stages on earth and the release of the spirit back into its true self and setting.

To be present at a passing and be able to see the transition take place is a privilege and a valued lesson. A former circle member Marie had become a much loved, dear friend. She suffered long the disease we term cancer. It spread and the affected parts of the physical body and the treatments to combat, took their toll. Life was terminating, slowly at first and when the spirit within called time on its carrier, the final stages came swiftly. The bedside vigil took place. Hands were held and soft words spoken to reassure we were staying by. The body began the process of release, breathing slowed and movements stilled. Quietness came over the room, only the clock ticked away the departure time.

Being what is termed a medium or sensitive, I first felt the temperature drop and the icy psychic breeze circulate around the room. Misty spirit forms including her husband and grandmother, were taking their place in readiness. In the hospice room the bright lights flooded every area and I felt sympathy for the spirit people entering this brilliance and how hard the difficulties were in adjusting to the setting. But they did, and all awaited the time. In less than five minutes swirling wreaths of energy began to form around the stomach or solar plexus area of the patient. I let go of her hands. Departure was imminent and must not be obstructed by the physical. My friend was making her entrance into spirit. The energy mass grew wider, spreading and encompassing the physical body and taking its shape, elevation had begun. Like a column of smoke, it rose, slowly, gently, peacefully. From the crown came a cord, similar to an umbilical cord, but finer in texture, grey/silver in colour and this stretched as the new energy-form spirit up-righted from its physical body. The spirit of her beautiful soul reached its full height, the cord released from the crown and the final breath made. I watched the spirit family step forward, gather around and take my friend up through what appeared to be the ceiling and solid walls. My gaze was fixed there for quite a while in wonder. How could I weep, what right had I to want their return to this earth and pain when their involvement with this earth plane had come to its natural end?

I had witnessed the expiry of a vehicle we term the body, the release of the spirit figure into the arms and care of spirit loved ones. I had seen them go home and soon looked forward to them paying a return visit. Outside the full moon was enormous and stars in abundance. What a wonderful evening for my friend's journey home. Within two weeks my friend visited during séance. It was a short visit as energy levels were still depleted through the long body illness, and spirit life was still being adjusted to. Visits are more regular now and I was shown her home in spirit, with the word's

"Kate, you said it would be beautiful, but beauty is too small a word." The scene presented was a valley of lush green growth, purple distance hills, a river running through the gorge and a white cottage by its banks. A lovely soul had earned its perfect place to stay as long as needed before continuing the journey of the soul.

ENERGY

WHAT IS ENERGY? The strength and vitality required for sustained physical or mental activity.

There are many words used in describing energy – strength, force, spark, effervescence, power, potency and drive to name but a few. A person's physical and mental powers are energy, which require energy to function correctly, as do all living organisms. This source of energy is mainly through our intake of food. In physics we are told that energy is a property, which must be transferred to a mechanism, in order for it to work – whether this is to heat the mechanism or to move it. The moving of an object is termed kinetic energy. Electric, magnetic, radiant energy (carried by light) and thermal energy (temperature) are collectively known as common energies. Civilisations require energies to survive and function and depend largely on fossil fuels, nuclear, and of late, renewable. The Earth's climate is driven by radiant energy, which it receives from the Sun and geothermal energy within the earth itself.

The above are a few references to energy, which to our earthly life, are incredibly useful if harnessed correctly and necessary for our continuance on this planet. For all its many forms and uses, energy is still hard to define.

To better understand a little more of the energies concerning the human body in connection to our spirit body, we must view the layers of energy fields with the importance of how they function in our daily lives and their effects in spiritual growth. Here follows a traditional schema starting from where the energy (aura) is closest to the physical body:

AURA – the coloured energy field emanation surrounding life.

The aura is a field of energy which emanates and vibrates from and surrounds your body, which can be perceived by sight and touch. The lower the vibration, the closer the energy is to the body, the higher the vibration the more it expands outward. Each person has a unique experience and perception of the aura depending on their level of spirit knowledge and awareness, which means some people, can see colour differences and the movements in the energy circulating around the outer, physical frame. Descriptions can never be exact as the aura is in a constant state of flux. Fluctuations occur in response to a person's mental, physical, emotional and spiritual states effecting these changes. Also responses to their environments and conditions of existences from past, present and future are all contained with the auric field.

Etheric Layer

According to tradition this is the aura's first energy layer. The densest part: the easiest to be visible as it extends about two inches proud of the physical body. This auric layer acts as a bridge between our physical and subtle bodies. It contains structures which allow us to absorb the spiritual power from the surrounding environment and to process it before it becomes part of the physical body. It also acts as a cast/template for the form which our physical body takes, and as such, retains its structure after the physical body has died (taken its transition). The etheric body or layer is blue/grey in colour and all chakras seen within it will also appear blue/grey.

Emotional Layer
This layer is associated with our feelings and emotions, which can be seen within it as swirling colours. Powerful, positive feelings tend to be clear and bright, while negative feelings or thoughts in turmoil, appear dark and muddy. Extremely pure emotional states show pastel hues. In the emotional layer chakras appear in their traditional colours.

Mental Layer
Thoughts and ideas appear within this layer as pulses of coloured lights (which vary in brightness according to the strength of the emotions behind each thought). This layer is often perceived as a bright yellow field around the head (the origin of haloes in artwork) and is captured easily by Kirlian photography.

Astral layer or body
This layer relates to our higher emotions of love and all the colours within it are tinted slightly pink. This is the highest frequency as it is from here that we connect with each other on an emotional level, often by way of extending cords emanating from the solar plexus

chakra to those with whom we have a close emotional connection. This aura is a bridge between the higher and lower physical energies, acting as a gateway between the higher and lower auric frequencies.

Etheric Temple or Higher Etheric body
This is a higher vibration of the etheric body. It looks a little like a photographic negative and is a type of mould/facsimile: energies coalesce here into the form that the lower layers of our aura and our physical body will take.

Celestial body also known as the higher Emotional body
This layer is the spiritual equivalent to the emotional layer/body. It is the gateway through which pure, unconditional love flows to us from the Universal mind and higher spiritual realms. When we are experiencing deep states of meditation, mystical ecstasy or certain levels of mediumship, this layer vibrates with great strength.

Ketheric Body (also known called the Spiritual Body)
The layer corresponding with our higher mental faculties appears like a golden egg-shaped shell which surrounds all the other layers. The term Ketheric is derived from Cabala where Kether (Hebrew for the Crown) is the highest sphere on the Tree of Life. This body layer holds information about our Life Path (our reason for incarnating into our present life), about our past lives and about our future path. Within this layer

are found the channels which allow us to draw into ourselves the healing energies of the Universe.

We are told by spirit in séance that the outer coloured energy fields surrounding the body correspond to the soul's energy emittance in what has been described as a "rainbow effect". Growth of the soul depicts changes in intensity of these energy rings becoming brighter, richer in colour and strength as progression takes the spirit further into the spheres of knowledge and awareness.

SPIRIT ENERGY

Now we turn to what is to ourselves the most important of all energies – Spirit Energy. In order to understand this better, we first need to know a little of the energy we are familiar with yet pay little attention to. For instance, when we flick a switch we expect a result, whether this is light, heat or entertainment. However, we cannot be so relaxed and acceptant when it comes to spirit energy. To evoke this energy requires respect, devotion, deep meaningful prayer and contemplation on the higher mind and realms, as this energy is carried by love, the love of God for all living things. It is not supernatural but rather natural – as it carries aspects of nature, and we are all of nature.

The amount and excellence of spiritual energy is determined by conditioning of the person that is stimulating it. For example, if the person gives little thought to the words uttered in supplication and has little focus, concentration or *ennui*, although this is better than no prayer at all, little of the spiritual energy will be forthcoming and therefore have little desired effect. On the other hand, if careful preparation is applied when getting oneself into the right mind set, if words are uttered from a heart full of love and devotion to God, and has only thoughts of serving others, then the deliberations and sentiments are transmitted in stronger waves and carried higher to the levels of more purposeful energy spheres, for valuable actions to be done in all regions and areas of the spirit worlds and the earth plane.

Spirit energy is the universal life force. Just as the common energies benefit the body and our living standards, so spiritual energy is the food of souls. The energy that we can induce by prayer, thought and deed can and is used by those in the spirit world, like energy stored in a battery pack. The spirit people are able to use this where and when needed, immediately or at a later time. The benefits of meditation to still the mind before prayer to the Supreme Being plus positive thought direction are powerful acts in evoking spirit energy.

WHAT ARE WE IF NOT ENERGY? *HUMAN ENERGY (LIFE)*

That beautiful fuel that can only be God-given and comes from the higher mind and its creative thought is the same energy that awakens a bulb, grows the stem, stirs the bud and opens the flower to give pleasure to our senses, feeding the insects who in turn feed us. All this originates from the energy that is called life. The cycle of birth and transition, whether this is human, animal, flora, fauna etc. follows a natural energy course. Through transition part of this energy is left on earth to help regenerate, but the other and more important part returns to spirit and takes its rightful place there. This energy, that cannot be extinguished, cannot be killed, has no concept of death, flows through every living thing on this planet. It is often misunderstood, overlooked, taken for granted and little known.

As we are energy, therefore, we can tap into energy. If we take time and give patience to ourselves, we can attune our being to the energies not only around us in all living things, but beyond to the very place from which we have come. This place has many titles, the spirit world, heaven, paradise, nirvana, etc., but in all these names the one resounding fact is that this place is HOME.

Just because we have left our homes for a short while, until we gain earthlier and bodily dwelling experience, it does not mean to say that the door to our spirit home is slammed shut and locked tightly when we leave. Rather there is no door but just a stronger, higher energy field that divides and which, for the most part, keeps the spirit (true self) in the confines of its carrier (the body) until it is fully ready to be released and is able to make the journey home again.

The use of the energy dividing the two worlds is not forbidden. It is there for us to experience, to learn from and to connect with, but sadly multitudes do not, and a valued lesson is lost. Connecting with the spirit energy while in the body is far from easy but truly worthwhile. This is the food of progression, evolvement and advancement in our spiritual quest, in order to grow and reach the higher planes of godliness, knowledge, happiness and fulfilment. This free-flowing energy has healing properties, mood enhancers, strength boosters, vitality and riches of happiness deeper than any material wealth. Our hunger and thirst for materialism hushes the force of this energy. We have lost the balance of what is our need, to rather what we crave. The wanting of plenty starves the soul of its vital fuels and we begin to lose the competence of engaging with what is our natural energy, whether this be earth or spirit based. Our material growth should enhance the spirit, each new step in technology is a gift and should be shared but we have created a King called commercialism – and finance sadly rules. As more is developed, our greed expands and we constantly discard what is not current, and fill the earth with despoil, the like of which the planet has never known and cannot sustain. The more we reach out for additions the farther we leave our spirit in deficiency.

RECEIVING ENERGY FOR THE PURPOSE OF MEDIUMSHIP

This energy varies greatly in the level and uses in mediumship. It is also personal to each individual and as we are all individual, I suspect the amount and quality of energy attracted to each medium is to a greater or lesser degree. Therefore, I can only speak of the energy that is attracted to me and the way it is felt when working with spirit beings.

When delivering clairaudience, clairvoyance and clairsentience, energy lighter than a breeze is felt. It brushes my hands, face, mouth and around the throat area. It is a cool ethereal caress, light as a summer's breeze, bringing joy within and I cannot suppress a smile. It engages with my solar plexus and that excited butterfly feeling arises with the expectancy of connecting with life beyond the earth. My right ear becomes red and hot to the touch; my hearing is sharpened. There is a twinning effect of being present yet being aware of another level of existence. As each spirit contact is made the cool breeze effect diminishes or increases depending on the spirit communicator's skill and their ability to accept and control the energy being used in this method of communication.

Through the spirit communicator, the switch between the three Clair's is made, again depending on their ability to use the faculties of clairvoyance, clairaudience or clairsentience. Generally, not all can use all three faculties, as the mastery of this takes time, effort, devotion and progression when in the spirit state. If the one wishing to communicate has very limited ability in their communication skills, then my controller – guide, helper whatever title is used for this spirit being, steps in and delivers the address. When the spirit guides are communicating there is a marked change in the strength and depth of energy and a stronger reaction is placed on my frame as their energies and personalities merge with mine, and I am half myself and half them. Over the years of working with spirit the recognition of their energies within my family, guides and controllers, has developed to the point where it is known in an instant. To explain fully – when my daughter telephones she does not say "Hello I am your daughter I was born in the month of March, I have blond hair, blue eyes, etc." – all that my daughter says when phoning is "Hi, it's me." The voice is immediately recognised. Likewise, each spirit's energy is instantly known because it has life, personality and individuality, (like a familiar knock on the door), their energy and presence is acknowledged and accepted readily without lengthy introduction.

When working with these teachers, it is vital to build recognition, a rapport and most importantly trust. When giving yourself in service to spirit work and the spirit world, you must have an understanding of the energies you are committing to and the degree and level of progression of the minds you will be engaging with. This practice should be uppermost when undertaking development of mind and body in readiness to dedicate oneself to the workings and deliverance of spirit energy.

Spirit energy is valuable and when used via the communication method, is very limited. I term it liquid gold. Every drop is precious and should be savoured as it is God-given, generated by the Universal Mind and gifted by spirit for the purpose of advancement of the soul. It should never, ever be taken lightly, nonchalantly or with indifference. The emphasis must be on respect, privilege and gratitude. Although there is an endless supply, however, when used through a vessel (medium), our time in this connection is not endless, as our bodies could not withstand the level of power and continuity. A time limit for receiving energy must be applied when used in mediumship, followed by refreshments, a period of rest or light duties. For example our séances are conducted on an evening twice weekly and last between one and a half hours to two hours.

ENERGY AND THE PHYSICAL MEDIUM

Ectoplasm/etheric energy drawn from the medium's body by the spirit operators, added to from their own sources and those present in the séance room is used and manipulated – producing the effect of physical phenomena. This energy can be created in many forms – visible and invisible – white or coloured, depending upon the results the spirit controllers wish to achieve with this amazing substance.

In physical mediumship the spirit operators use an abundance of etheric energy and matter in order to produce various manifestations. They do this exactly through the directed use of mind – first releasing this energy/matter from the physical medium's body. Most often, although not always, the medium is in a state of deep trance, allowing the spirit operators to work with, and manipulate, this etheric energy/matter. During materialization of spirit, the medium usually sits within an enclosed area, called a cabinet. This helps focus the energies and creates a type of battery from which the phenomena can be built and energized. There is usually a curtain in front of the cabinet holding in the energy until it has built sufficiently enough for it to be released. At this point the curtain can be parted in order for the sitters and guests to see the workings within the cabinet and for the energy to be expelled into the séance room. The energy conditions of physical mediumship dictate it to be operated in darkness (blacked out conditions) or with a dim red light providing the only light source. Spirit informs us that white light infiltrates and breaks down the energy whereas red light affects in the same way but to a lesser degree. Also the room will serve better in holding the energy if used solely for the purpose of physical phenomena.

Although the above descriptions are only general

guidelines, some amazing phenomena have been documented using white light. However, these are exceptional, in the minority, and it is generally accepted that in order to gain the best out of physical mediumship, darkened/blacked out/or red-light séances are the most effective.

The aim and that of everyone experiencing this earthly path, is to evolve sufficiently, as to have merit to receive the highest of spiritual energy and the light, expansion and love which always accompany this.

UNBROKEN LINKS

The work with spirit continues up to the time of writing in 2022, unlike our material employment there is no retirement. Spirit work and awareness becomes a way of life, working in and around our material activities. Like a fine wine it ages well. As the body and mind mature so does the strength and connections with the higher realms. Years of practice and contact strengthen bonds and cements working techniques, forging a smoother flow of energy, proof and knowledge. There is no prejudice of age in the spirit worlds, rather it is embraced and shows the soul in a progressive light.

Greta, a sitter of many years, emigrated (see chapter 7, River in Flow). Together with her husband Rev. John Lilek, who was an experienced physical medium, they travelled throughout his homeland of USA, spreading the work and love of spirit. Now John has made his spirit journey through transition, Greta continues the work. In doing so she creates a bridge of energy between us, cancelling out the earth miles from the USA to the UK.

A short while ago Greta kindly presented me with a trumpet instrument through which spirit voices were amplified during many séances along with the tape cassettes recording them. This trumpet has a long history of working from the 1920's to 2014 throughout the USA with various mediums, including her husband John, during his own séances and together in séances held by

Rev. James (Jim) G Tingley. It is commendable and an honour for me to house. It sits in my spirit room, joining in our 'present day' séances and at times attracting its former users. The times when the Reverend John and Reverend James link into the séances held here, our collective energies allow union, and we become a unit in the work of spirit.

Spirit's past work through this trumpet is inspiring. Listening to their recorded voices brings you into the séance rooms held at that time. Encouraging words given by spirit are not just for those who were present but have meaning for us all.

Hence, I have included here two short extracts from séances by Reverend J G Tingley prior to his passing in 1999 and John's in August 2014. As a brief introduction – The Reverend James G Tingley's mediumship was exceptional. He grew up in Eaton Rapids, Michigan. At the age of 12 Jim Tingley became interested in psychic matters. By the age of thirteen he had read intensively large amounts of printed materials relating to spirit communication. At 15 he was in high demand to deliver accurate evidential spirit messages both in public and private. He was ordained by the National Spiritual Association age 16 and given his own church in Jackson, Michigan shortly after. Jim later developed physical mediumship, from trumpet work, to independent voice, to full materialisation of spirit, sometimes three or four spirits solidly building at one time, on occasion without Jim being in trance. Other phenomena accompanied Jim throughout his life displaying rare and remarkable abilities of contact with spirit. His work attracted large gatherings from the humble to royalty and was named

USA's most tested medium. In his later years in (1992) The National Spiritual Association presented him with the President's Award for his 54 years of distinguished service. Dr. Rev J G Tingley was an accomplished speaker and teacher, taking the Rev. John Lilek under his wing to become his student and follower in his footsteps.

*****

Medium – Dr. Rev. J G Tingley D.D. – in trumpet séance recorded 10/9/1989 – Present – Rev. John Lilek and invited guests (unnamed) – This extract is only a small amount taken from the many contacts during this sitting and kindly granted for its publication by my good friend Greta Lilek of Bucksport Maine USA:

Extract: *Spirit voice of Mabel:*

You are a natural sensitive of the spiritual vibration of God and we are here with you to help. I will teach you the following in preparation for your further development in mediumship.

Always ask the Divine Spirit to bring unto you a peace of mind that you may develop the wonderful gift of mediumship and only use the gift for the betterment of mankind and for the helping agent of goodness. Try to the best of your ability not to become discouraged. You are a child of God and so desire the higher teachings of God, which is truth. Obey the Laws of Nature both physical and spiritual. The virtue of patience is necessary for your unfolding. Have faith always, as faith is a substance, a substance of a belief in God and a substance which is evidential to His manifestations. Feel the flowing through you of God's power and accept this from the bottom of your feet to the top of your head. Ask God to unlock your Chakras and for them to move in harmony in order to give and receive. Thank God for all experiences in what you are going to be and become.

Dr. Reverend J G Tingley D.D. USA – Direct voice medium in séance 21/09/1989 – amongst those present Rev. John Lilek, Rev. Ann Hart and invited guests.

Spirit voice of Mabel:

Know this of yourselves: – To the fire of God, I command that all sinister forces leave forever for I am a perfect child of God and through my instrumentality I will be and become that great part of the Spirit that never ends and knows no death.

I am the breath of the morning wind, the fragrance of the morning flower. I am the freshness in the morning dew and I shall see my way and path myself to the greatest trails of adventure. With the recognition of all my guides and teachers at my side. We are following the way of spirit where there is no destiny called end, it just begins all over again. It is evolving and revolving. It is extending and gives lending, blending the beautiful hues of the rainbow and it is therein I shall find my pot of gold and so will it be. Forget your past errors and live anew. Let soul growth be the way for you.

Balancing the Wheel

During the séances it was stressed several times by the spirit guides in their teachings to Rev John that balance in all things is essential. They used the expression of 'Balancing the Wheel'. I concur with this as balance in life's work, pleasures and spirit contact is indeed essential. Rest and eating small portions of fresh food that nourish as opposed to one large meal are necessities when preparing, to work for spirit. Moderation in all things is the key to balancing mind and body. It is within all mediums the urge to take on too much, especially in the beginning of development. We want to serve and offer as much help as possible to those wanting reassurance or looking for help through spirit messages. This reduces the mind and body to becoming over tired, leading to depletion of both physical and spirit energies. One outcome of this is mood swings wherein thoughts of not progressing or worries of receiving a small number of messages etc. become fixed. These thoughts can interfere or temporarily stop development. Although the séance extract given to Rev. John was mainly of help and advice for his mediumship, the message is relevant for all especially budding mediums and at times we should all try to 'Balance the Wheel'.

During our present-day séances, it is wonderful to share golden moments together and keep the links with spirit secure. To shake hands across the fence of energy dividing earth from the spirit worlds. To touch the higher elevation of spiritual happiness and be one in the union of spirit, no matter how long the length of time has passed. It is an opportunity to bring mind to mind, heart to heart, beating out the sound of love. Love that crosses all divides bringing spirit people, human people and worlds together, allowing the continuance of soul growth and the energies that feed.

PERSPECTIVE

THOUGHTS

Sadly, I find the portrayal of spirit by some branches of the entertainment field tedious and at times irresponsible, especially when, through their work, youngsters are drawn into what is called by some 'The Occult'. There are levels of energy all around us and in each layer, spirit life. If a young inexperienced mind opens a door to the lower energy forms, a potential danger awaits. Like attracting like is a certainty and through curiosity, ignorance or thrill-seeking some involve themselves in the undertaking of contacting 'ghosts' without the full concept of what or whom they are attracting. If their venturing is one of wicked intent, mischief making or of actions with the purpose of controlling or frightening others, a rebound is more often imposed on themselves as the lower energy spirit forms attach and manipulate ignorant and unguarded, immature human beings. Opening the door to spirit without prior knowledge in the techniques, safety and disciplines can be costly. Energy is a force that must have respect and caution.

What was written in times gone by of hauntings resulting in limited fear has now extended to spectres so horrific and has pushed our true selves when in 'spirit' into fiendish apparitions. I feel certain the fear instilled by these uneducated attempts of description, although giving brief amusement, do little in uniting us with the spirit worlds in what is and should be, a natural coexistence. We are intelligent enough to know that our loved ones, our children and cherished friends, having passed on before us, would not suddenly turn into haunting, possessing ghoulish monsters. Yet what has been said, seen or read instils deep within (once myself included) the initial fear of ghosts, spirits and possible hauntings. Through this fear we deny ourselves the continued presence and love that these wonderful beings are so eager to give. We are told by some religions of the wrong to 'meddle' with spirits – 'Work of the devil' and so on. They teach of the Holy Spirit and His love for us, yet deny the means of contact, and demand that the only right way to gain access to God is by sitting in man-made temples listening to preaching and doing as is said. If attending places of religion brings some of the comfort or solace you are seeking – then continue. However, no religion has the authority to control, cleanse souls, guarantee heaven, instil guilt and make fearful the expectation of hell for our human failings. We are spirit and will always be spirit. We are responsible for our own soul growth, experiences, achievements and accountability for our misdemeanours. We answer to the Natural Spiritual Law, not to any belief system that has been manufactured by man for his own greed or gratification over many years. Rich or poor, weak or strong, religious or atheist, at the point of transition (death) of the body, transition occurs and the spirit, your spirit, lives on to begin the next phase in your development. In the spirit spheres we do not sit idle, there is too much to see, do and experience. There is no

RIP but rather PIP – Progression in Peace.

I admit my good fortune at being chosen by Little Raven and others. Their guidance in the early phases of my development, soon altered any concept of 'ghosts' and turned fear into ordinariness when meeting with those disengaged of the body. The correct techniques in procuring safety, at each séance, the setting ajar of the door to the spirit realms, thus enabling communication and love to flow, were their lessons. Through patience and teachings, ingrained fears of ghosts melted away and acceptance of spirit, family and friends embraced. If you fear spirit, then you fear yourself for we are all of spirit. Unchanged by death, the person you are remains. You are what you will always be, a forever evolving energy, whether this energy is in the flesh or in the spirit.

We do not go to spirit, without first coming from spirit. In the outer realms lie our natural state and placement. While in this earth form, the outer casing is made from earth's elements with its contributions allowing function on the earth plane. The spirit functioning within this enclosed framework is of a finer substance, with origins and materials from and attuned to the spirit realms. The solidity felt on earth through the body is transferred into the spirit at transition. In the spirit state and world, what corresponds to solid is solid. To the touch liquid remains a flowing substance. Structures stand firm and growth abounds in its customary process. In this heightened state of naturalness clarity is given, not only of sight and the other senses, but of mind. The puzzles, misgivings and apprehensions regarding transition and life beyond are there for all to understand. The passing of a spirit and its entry back into the spirit world receives the opening to evolve. This short earth time of bodily living is to gather knowledge and experiences to add to that evolvement. Our status on the earth plane regarding our soul's progression is either in infant schooling, junior or senior with the objective of reaching higher educational levels. On the discarding of the body, we enter back into what should be, The University of Spirit, for our education to continue. A combination of theory, practical and pleasure are lessons taken in all manner of subjects and are open to all as a means to aid the soul's fulfilment. Each task is undertaken in love and joyous service of the Divine, for the benefit of others and ourselves. We do not sit idle, and just as the realm we will enter in, we are drawn to the work, activities and pleasures according to that realm and our spiritual growth. If awareness of the spirit planes and some of its teachings were known to more, acceptance to be part of the system and a willingness to offer service to that system would benefit all mankind while living out our experiences on earth and would better prepare each individual for what is undoubtedly the inevitable.

The accounts thus far will hopefully give the reader a glimpse of my interactions with the spirit world and some of its inhabitants in the company and guidance of Little Raven and others. In doing so there is nothing unique, special or extraordinary. The ability is there for everyone, with or without education, religion or any formal training. Ourselves as spirits are temporarily encased in a physical body, yet are active, free and awaiting direction. The controller in this is self. You are the trigger point. You are the awakening mechanism with the starting key being made by thought. Once the stirring of our inner being commences, an unfolding of knowledge and development begins to take place. It is then down to each individual how that development will be undertaken. Usually, the first steps are in questioning and seeking answers, research and reading matter or being present at an event, such as a clairvoyant demonstration. This being done and curiosity satisfied, many return to their mode of living, giving little or no thought to their own development or future life in spirit.

As with most people seeking proof of their loved one's survival of so-called death, it is at the reliance of others, (mediums) often strangers and in unfamiliar surroundings, adding to one's fear and anxiety. I hope these lines of writing will encourage you to become less of a spectator and more of a participant. We cannot go on relying on others to do the work for us. Opening the door to spirit and the higher realms and vibrations are a duty each one should undertake. A larger body of awareness and the collective energy that this will bring, will give the earth the equilibrium so badly needed and ourselves a firm understanding of the merits of personal progression, together with acceptance of those already in the spirit state and a readiness for our own spirit form to come. Research into outer space is commendable and brings added knowledge to mankind. But the need for inward research is greater. The exploration of mind and what mind can achieve and reveal, unlocks the door to our true spiritual advancement. Life beyond our world awaits and is accessible only when in the spirit body but contact and communication is possible while in the flesh state through the language common to each, the language of thought. Until we collectively become trained in the usage and understand the capabilities our minds hold, and what our amalgamation of energies can accomplish, our spirit, when occupying the body, will remain stunted and undeveloped.

In a short space of time our world has exploded with technology, and we are able to see and speak to our fellows on all of earth's continents and when in outer space. However, few have the skills or confidence to speak or see those who are much closer, as the curtain dividing ourselves from spirit, proves for most, difficult to accept and to part. For those who have lifted the curtain and know and work with spirit, I commend you. For those who have yet to do so, your spirit self and your teachers await.

Thank you for walking with me through my spiritual course thus far. May I wish, when walking yours all the love and joy of spirit.

PART 3

Spirit Speaks

CHILD'S WISDOM

Some spirit beings, having passed as a child, prefer to stay in a childlike state when communicating with the earth people, because a spirit child lessens the fear of spirit contact and can be more readily accepted. Communicators can have a child's voice and stature but sometimes when speaking can drop in adult information, one such is Lucy, a regular at séance. The following pieces of information kindly given by Lucy during her regular séance visits is in the hope that her explanations may simplify the process of moving the soul forward when in its natural state of spirit life.

These extracts are taken from six séances held in my home 2020 to 2021:

Spirit controller Lucy:

> I am not knowledgeable to a high degree as everyone here has to learn and I have much to comprehend and experience, but so far I have learnt that the quickest way to go forward is through acceptance and connecting with the spirit worlds especially when in the body state. Then, when your spirit is released from the body, and you come back into the spirit self, it is more easily achievable to link with other dimensions

or with those who dwell in higher levels of existence, if acceptance and knowledge of the spirit world has been achieved first. I will use my child's explanation and say that progression is like a step ladder, you have to start at the bottom and when there, if you totally, totally reject spirit connection, possibilities, communication or our very presence, when you come out of your body and enter into what is your spirit body, which is the first step on the ladder, you cannot progress further because of your previous rejections and therefore you have to come back into the body to try again.

The first step of the ladder is what you call the Astral. While in the Astral state you reach a stage where you want to go on (progress) and it is then that you begin to understand that in order to progress you have to go back and learn the acceptance of spirit, especially that of your own. If the spirit in question rejects going back into the body, it is rather like a goldfish in a bowl not going anywhere, just going round and round and round. It will try and leap out but that is not the way to survive, so the fish must go back to the place where it can survive and likewise a spirit coming back into the body to learn the ways of progression, is its survival in the manner of how it should and was intended to be. Therefore, key elements of the progression of the soul/spirit at this time of evolvement can only be obtained in flesh form.

When knowledge is obtained you can progress

up your steps 3, 4, 5, and achieve a beautiful plane of existence or whatever you wish to call your rightful place that you have earned for yourself. Progression here is at a pace to suit each individual. There are no hardships to endure, no temptations or any of the burdens a human body encounters but we do still need to learn and overcome difficulties each lesson presents. It is here where you yourself will make the choice of coming back to the earth and into body as a way of furthering yourself. You will not be at the bottom of your ladder again as you have already surpassed this, but rather take on the role as a helper of spirit, a worker for spirit, not just for your own spirit this time but for others whether they listen or not – and more importantly be a communicating bridge for the spirit world and those there who work with the earth plane on all levels, all in the interest of progression.

When again you have completed your time on earth in this way and have returned to spirit, you can rise up your step ladder of progression quicker perhaps to steps 6,7,8 and there explore even more the beauties and wonders of our creation. You are still at liberty to go to your previous existence (level 5 or lower) and enjoy what is there and the companionships formed. It is by progression you are given the freedom to explore, expand the mind and savour all aspects of your true self and in the spheres which are deserving of your spirit's advancement.

In speaking the truth I do not know how many

levels or spheres there are because I have not seen the top of my ladder yet, but I do know that there are, what I call bright shiny beings that emit light of such brilliance, it is impossible to express. They are in a higher state of growth that dictates levels of light and purity that is only accessed by the evolvement of spirit by many practices, experiences and knowledge that accompany a soul's forward journey. Some of these advance beings were like myself once and progressed through flesh and had the experiences that accompany that state but some have not had a pathway linked to the body but have taken other ways of progression. This I know maybe difficult to understand but the energy in spirit is manufactured in all ways and is governed by creative minds and mind in the spirit form has more liberty for expansion unlike the confinement of the body, providing it is linked to the soul's advancement.

*****

Choices in the spirit worlds are not always readily accepted – as with the earth plane – free will applies:

> Some spirit people keep in their places of living for long periods. These places are not in the Astral as you term it. They have accepted transition of their soul and have an understanding of having left the earth plane, but they are happy to dwell where they are. However, when the bright shiny advanced ones come into their realms in order to teach and speak to them, some choose not to

attend because they do not accept anything other than the place where they are, just like when they were on the earth plane. Some do attend and listen but think what they have heard is incorrect, again because their place in spirit is very real, just like the earth plane and they cannot see beyond it. Others however, that listen, begin to think, and have thoughts of 'it must be true, there must be more than this place'. This then becomes the spark that ignites, which in turns becomes brighter because they begin to search and listen more and gain knowledge, the knowledge of progression.

One must practice the art of widening your thoughts, as the possibilities are great and wondrous in what the mind can achieve, especially when free of the body. Out of the body means you become the real you. Lives would not be destroyed in grief if more knew of the spirit life to come.

*****

When we are working with people still on the earth, our reward for doing so is at times to visit a higher level and experience life there for a brief period. This gives us the encouragement to advance ourselves. The place where I live now is beautiful, but beauty is not perfection and so can always be improved. We must call these places 'worlds' because of the vastness and diversity of life there. Then you must try to comprehend that each one place is much much larger than your earth world. This is why some people when gaining access to a place they say "I like this world. I do not have to work in this world, it is full of beauty and therefore I am staying." But there is always more to come.

I rather like progress, and this is why I come back to work, this time not in the flesh but as a communicator, but when I reach a certain 'step' and gain the choice of whether to return to the earth or not, then I will speak to those who are teaching me. Sometimes the Teachers come to people on a certain level of advancement and say would you consider going back to another level or even into the body? These higher beings have an overview of all worlds, and if some spheres are really not progressing as they should, then individuals are asked to help with this. The Teachers need workers to communicate through in order to help with the standard of progression. They give you a long period of thinking, and you may say, I wish to help but I am so comfortable with those who are my immediate friends that I would be unhappy to leave them, and in these circumstances a collective spirit family group will descend together. Although there may be just one in the group who will act as a communicator (medium) for spirit, the others will have a life and time of experiences. These are taken in thought back to the spirit worlds so that the higher beings can understand the conditions of the earth plane or other planes at this time. If necessary, implementing procedures to help move life forward in the process of evolvement. It is of little point having wonderful inventions to help make life on all levels more pleasing, if the spirit itself is not responding to development.

I have tried to simplify my description of how you, when in the body and in the spirit, can progress, hopefully without offending you by these simplifications. To use a child's description of how things are seen is often more acceptable, especially when we are trying to explain and convince minds of an invisibility to you, but a real and solid creation to us.

*****

I can chat away in most conditions but when the conditions are right, my voice is more fluent and stronger as I can hold the vibration longer. More of my personality is able to come through and therefore conditions set out for spirit communication is important for every contact with the spirit world. When the room and settings are right and the level of welcome also, then we can be ourselves in the truest sense. It is in the acceptance, not by just expressing hello, but how you feel inside when addressing a spirit (no fear or apprehension) as we can feel the uncertainty and nervousness. But in time when fear is overcome, we know then that we are accepted as family and friends and greeted accordingly, this puts ourselves at ease and the communication process becomes natural. If I could take you to my place now and you would meet people there, they would not say "Oh my, I have seen someone in the body!" We do not become frightened at seeing the bodily form as you are frightened at a spirit form. We just accept that you are back amongst us. While in the body, you as a spirit visit for long periods and more importantly come to replenish, but in earth time terms the stay is short. Eventually the pull back to the earth becomes stronger as the higher self knows there is still a task to be completed, experiences to encounter before the visit to the spirit world becomes permanent. It is customary for you to pop into spirit and pop back at regular intervals, especially in the periods of sleeping the body. It is as normal as me being here speaking to you now.

*****

Question from a sitter: "When in spirit is it easier to help someone already known to you when in the body, rather than a stranger?"

In my experience it is the former as recognition is readily there and hopefully trust is there also. The person of concern may be in a situation where they are amenable to listening and accept your help this time, whereas you may have tried to help them previously without success either while on the earth or in the spirit world. When you have planted a thought or given a suggestion it is better to leave them a little while to absorb your assistance. However, if there is no success then you are at liberty to seek help from your teachers/guides and say I have tried to help my friend but without a response. They may encourage you to try something else or indeed wait until the thought goes out that help is required. It is a matter of coaxing and gaining trust and when achieved you can encourage the friend to come with you and you can show them a better place, where they are more comfortable, less apprehensive and begin to adjust and want to understand more. They may feel a little uneasy at not trusting you initially but that has no importance to you, the important thing is help has been given and accepted. You have gained their interest enough for them to move forward. If the spirit person you are trying to help is not known to you at all then this is quite a challenge for both. But if this work is what you wish to do as part of your soul development, opportunities to do so will arise. Souls in need of help have all manner of reasons as to why they are unable to move forward – fear, former religions, even the highly educated while on earth encounter difficulties in acceptance of their present situation. It is something that they have to adjust to either with help or in their own way and stages in development.

*****

Whenever we speak to you during our meeting times [séances] there are always spirit people taking an interest in our conversations and for some it may be of help, and in turn they act upon it and begin to seek ways of advancing. There is always a mixed audience at times of meeting with the earth so as to give an opportunity to experience communication methods and to ask questions regarding their own progressive abilities. It may give a timid spirit person the courage to send a thought out for help, give them an opening to listen a little more or take two steps forward away from the place they do not really want to be in. The meetings of earth and the spirit worlds not only opens a door into both our worlds but gives many in spirit the opportunities of discovery.

WHEN LIGHT IS SEEN

WHEN WE SEE LIGHT – WE SEE PROGRESSION

How communication is undertaken from the Unseen Worlds:

As with any finely tuned instrument it must be played by a proficient instrumentalist in order to achieve its fullest effect. To become proficient takes perseverance and love of the occupation. The tireless love of the spirit workers has proven time and time again how proficient they are in their communication skills and are finely tuned to the earth-plane's vibrations and the instruments (mediums) they have chosen to work with. Here are a couple of examples:

Spirit controller (White Eagle) speaking during séance –

> When we see light emanating from a soul, we see progression. This then becomes our love, our purpose, our occupation. We are about the business of progressing ourselves and others. How do you progress in the spirit world one might ask? This should come naturally by thinking – using your minds – curiosity. Thoughts are being created and minds are opening more by the methods of inspiration, creativity and motivation. Just as education begins by curiosity on the earth plane,

so it continues in the spirit worlds. Firstly, this occurs individually and a journey in discovery begins. Then there is connection, a coming together of 'like-minded' spirits, collectively for a purpose and when we are combined in the same thought and resolve, we have stronger potential and therefore our intention is greater. We have a larger endeavour to complete each phase of work that we have designed ourselves to do. Yes, we can produce the intention and energy when we are solo, but so much more if we combine, as there is greater intensity. However, we must emphasize it is not the number or volume that carries the effect, if the quality and worth is absent. The gathering of numbers must be conducive to merit the task. We can number five beings and produce notable power, ability and illumination and then we can number one hundred and five and have dimness, lack of strength and balance because there is deficiency in commitment, purpose and enthusiasm or the energies are not conducive to merge in a constructive manner. It is always trial and adjustment, just as on the earth plane or in any plane.

We can ready ourselves to draw close to an individual who initially expressed willingness to work for the souls' advancement, then subsequently, a short period passes, and the person becomes lethargic and emits "Oh I am not progressing," and so moves on to try something else. Here we see a soul struggling with patience and as has yet little understanding that to work with those connected to the spheres of stronger, more powerful energy; dedication and practice is required on both sides in developing the art of mediumship or to be in an intermediate state.

It is for spirit to understand too the difficulties faced when spirit is in the body condition and the need to blend with a personality that is agreeable to enter the state of servitude, allegiance and to stay steadfast in the cause of advancement. This undertaking is not without demands and adjustments, as the obligations made are for all spirit and the greater advance, whether this is in the earth body or in the outer spheres of the spirit worlds.

The individual and spirit when compatible must have the essentials to move forward together, for it is not possible for one to out stride the other, in the efforts to achieve and expand the areas of communication. Intermediary service should never stand still; there is no pinnacle in mediumship, only continued advancement. Communication is but one aspect of how we develop as individuals and collectively. Other forms of our development (as in your world) are through the arts, science, creation, growing and tending all life forms and immeasurably much more. As we do not have the limitations of materialism and a body expressing itself in age or illness, our opportunities for advancing the soul are wider, and more so, if we have gained knowledge through incarnation, not only of the earth plane but via the levels attributed to the spirit worlds and those beyond.

It is to be remembered that the visual and audible work being carried out in séance rooms on earth are only part of the work conducted by the spirit participants. We use the opportunity of communication for its good to be done on both sides, that is to say, we conduct ourselves in a classroom or as we have commented before, in an auditorium, so that those in the spirit spheres embarking on the road of communicating have, under the guidance of their teachers, an opportunity to observe how expression is formed, conducted, achieved or when the energy has disturbance, instability or fragility from either the earth or the spirit planes, the connection depletes, becomes distorted or expires. They learn the consistencies in energies, to respect its flow and strength. When a student has advanced somewhat, on occasion, permission is given for them to draw close to the medium to understand the difficulties of acceptance, management and blending of personalities of a spirit's into the vessel's energy field. All these things are tried, practised, governed in the spirit world in order to prepare the spirit communicators in readiness to connect with a willing spirit while in the body state, or in a higher spirit state, so both can develop complex transition methods of thought and the transfer of energy through energy without incurring harm to either party.

A Sitter asked Little Raven: "How do you connect with a soul willing to work for development?"

Little Raven replied by explaining that the intentions of a person's willingness to become a communicator prior to their reincarnation and the expressions and advancements this will give as part of their growth pattern, are indicated by themselves and acknowledged by their guides and teachers:

> Therefore, we begin by following the programme already designed before the soul agreed its bodily condition. This relates to the spirit's progressive level, as to the strength of power which can be given and used for communication, healing, audible or visual processes on the plane you call earth. Throughout the soul's body-growth and experiences, the level of energy is increased if – and we do say 'if' the soul is willing to advance. Most are happy to have limited power transfer which is often used in the giving and receiving of message communication during clairaudience or similar forms. The power strength increases for healing and during séance work. As gravity is the force of attraction that pulls together, so do we have the same method to connect with the structure of the vessel's (medium's) body. The gravity force in our spirit world has less weight and more speed as the spirit form has less density but the principle is the same. Just as you, we too have energy and force to keep us within the sphere of our evolution.

When working in earth conditions our energy makeup is altered and adjusted to meet the settings, otherwise our gravity force would pull us back into our own spheres. As the earth-pull sits heavier on our spirit frames, lessons in holding our build and shape in this environment, are lengthy before we can connect with a willing medium.

In spirit those interested in the commitment of any form of energy transfer are schooled intensely in the art, also, they are made to understand, respect and value each connection with the many realms engaged with progression and development. Sadly, when a soul enters the body form for a material earth life, we are seeing less training and preparation in the approach to spirit communication and the transmitting of energy. For the atmosphere or mental state conveyed in the earth's environment of wishing for the instant! Prevails. Creating an atmosphere of desiring mediumistic abilities, yet giving little time and effort to its study. For both divisions of earth and the spirit worlds, this problem must be worked through as our laws that govern connection, have limitations and cannot produce instant results. Man invented time and adopts the method of counting any progress by the calendar and the clock. Our method is the development of all being's immortal element, through the many changes of experience, growth in mind, character, moral strengths and more, which cannot be rushed or be part of the immediate. Finding solutions to problems is the added interest in our connecting with any sphere and pleasure savoured when success is gained and shared. Before I take my leave, I must speak a little on how, at times, the causes on the earth-plane affect the spirit planes. Humans living out their earthly lives think their actions are all about the earth, but this is not so – actions whether positive or negative reflect and one affects the other. The negatives issuing from the earth-plane make people in the spirit-planes anxious and concerned enough to make them aware that they can play a part in working for the betterment, for example, how to project and direct positive energy to counterbalance the negative, how to neutralize the effects of lower energy thoughts and replace with healing uplifting energy, above all, the importance of love and prayer. By these acts the more strength of energy we accumulate in the spirit worlds, it reaches the higher planes and a response there is caused. Without the positivity of prayer, thought, action, the higher realms are less aware of occurrences affecting the earth, especially the instability of war. So when negativity is created on the earth, you are not left to address the balance alone, reaction is underway on all levels in our worlds, to engage in and are added to one's progression. Never think of the earth as being solitary, there are greater minds and forces at work. The journey of the soul growth is long and must be so for all the lessons to be learnt. The human form housing the spirit at times gets a little ahead of itself and the need for it to be checked occurs. Discipline seems harsh but necessary otherwise wildness occurs, and in-turn becomes uncontrollable. Respect, learning and knowing must return when in the human state. We know the earth-plane weeps at times. It is with sadness that we have come to this stage in what we term modern times, awakening times as this should not be so. The human condition has come far in its evolving process and should aid the soul's development, not forget it, override it, or cease to listen to the spirit within"

GROWING THE SOUL

As previously written the purpose of earth living is the unfurling and development of the soul and the many facets it contains.

The following are sequences given (over many months) of recorded séances in my home by the spirit White Eagle via voice box communication. His teachings were given to the regular sitters and invited guests. The words of White Eagle will hopefully take the reader a little more into the ways and methods of spirit work when souls are at the beginning of spiritual growth or further along the road of progression. His helpful hints and suggestions given will inform of the importance of the soul's development.

Controller White Eagle:
The opening of the soul means acceptance. The acceptance of who you are. What experiences are needed to further the soul in its quest to be improved enough to gain access to the higher realms of consciousness that lie beyond incarnations and dwell in the totality of godliness. It is likened to being given a multitude of full-length mirrors to look at you, from every angle. To see yourself in past lives, in the present and what needs to be undertaken and recognized in

existences to come. To begin to see your pathway clearly, differently and be fascinated at each image presented so you come to want and need more of yourself, and the individual you are striving to be. In this human condition it is likened to being a fruit, you are here to ripen, become sweeter with knowledge until the whole of you begins to bloom inside and out.

Knowledge comes in many forms and not always by the written word. Compassion, loving all life forms, sickness, wealth, poverty, freedom, confinement, regret, hope and much more offer the growing soul opportunities to develop. It is how you express yourself, conduct yourself in each situation offered that contributes to the soul's elements. A difficult situation overcome strengthens the mind, forms the character and gives resolve to carry on. As you invigorate so will you energize others, they will feel your enthusiasm that penetrates and stirs feelings. We call this 'light', not the artificial light created on earth but the swelling of feelings, euphoric, a bliss that makes the human body feel buoyant, laugh, sing and embraces all with love and true affection. Our connection with you in the human state is to carry the light, carry the energy and the words of spirit so as to support and encourage. We are always drawing to the light and love within each evolving soul. It is felt by us so profoundly, like the beating heart we feel the pulse of happiness for each soul finding its pathway and determined to stay its course.

*****

Whatever is done on the earth plane affects both sides of the veil as we are designed and linked. If advancement is being generated, we share the positives. If disruption is being sought and implemented, we feel the negative and work is undertaken to keep this at bay so as not to interfere or disrupt the constructive elements that make the spirit worlds. It is difficult to visualise and accept the spirit within or the higher self, connected but apart, linked yet independent, when all you see is the flesh, all you feel is skin, muscle, bone all governed by a functioning brain. We do not wish to demean your intelligence but we try to simplify our explanations so you may understand some of the complexities and the freedoms offered when your true self emerges, and the human state is no longer beneficial. The mirror is always reflecting the solid being, which is corresponding to earth's conditions. From the spirit side of life, your higher self also views the reflection, wrapped in a material, flesh, but does not see the true solid, only the conditioning. The higher self can enter into the flesh at any time and link with you and the spirit self, to participate in any activity to gain experience and knowledge, then leave, returning to the vibration and state of living you have collectively achieved, there to oversee the work and progress your lower self is undertaking. The higher-self, governs, helps, assists, leads and guides. It belongs – it is you, an extension of you, as you are an extension of your higher self, a facet in a diamond undergoing just one of the many experiences you will gain on earth. The spirit within you can step out of the flesh to energize itself or rest away from the body and earth's heavy confines. The connection will always remain via the cord. This cord is not rigid and can stretch as far as you wish it to go. It will only break at the death separation when the physical is no more beneficial. Your spirit can travel to its higher self for advice at times when the brain overrides the intended path and carves a course that is detrimental to your progression. Then both the higher mind and the spirit self will join to steer or try to steer the lower self, back to the intended path. There are always complexities in the physical world when dealing with the spirit self and the mind when encased in flesh and a mind alongside a brain governing the body's physical actions. But to gain advancement and development of the soul – the spirit, mind, brain and body combined offer the necessities to do this."

*****

When given an energy form as a helper:

White Eagle – At previous meetings we have covered the topic of energy and once again, dear friends, we refer to energy and its application. Through contact with the spirit world you may be given various gifts (you think symbolically), including the gift of an animal. When this occurs it is often in relation to past alliances. During one or more episodes on the earth plane you may have worked with this animal, loved this animal and likewise when in the spirit realms, shared many experiences together.

Yet now when in the earthly state, all memory of this has dulled. You may refer to the animal as only figurative if you wish, but more often than not there is much more than imagery as you are renewing an acquaintance of love, of working and of being in true harmony with each other. They may not share a voice similar to your own but the voice they give to your mind will be understood, just as the words were uttered from a human voice.

Take the whole of the meaning when given an animal. Do not make the mistake of accepting the helper just with words of gratitude, but rather expand the mind to cover its potential. Love the gift as it will love you, work with the gift as it will work alongside you and the benefit of doing this will be for both sides. Look deep within its energy for all its virtues. Each animal has in-built qualities – strength, courage, movement, colour, loyalty, companionship and affection.

Interact with these features and the vibration between you will flow and strengthen. Remember not all gifts are of the human/spirit being kind, but they are just as important to your development and understanding of the energy of spirit. Just as in an animal, a rose or other gifts of blooms can evoke feelings and memories. Their colour and design can uplift and once implanted in your thoughts, unlike an earth's flowering will not wither or fade, unless it lies dormant within the mind. Therefore, at intervals awaken the gift whatever it may be, stir the life there, for energy is life and life is energy. This theme needs to be adopted and understood more, so I encourage you to work with your gift and let it respond, so both will gain and advance. When this is done an understanding of the relationship, which was formed in times past and is still being formed, will become clearer. You will find more and more within your gift when you begin to explore it yourself."

*****

Development:

We cannot emphasize enough the importance of development while on the earth as this propels you further through the spheres of the spirit planes, meriting the advancing soul. Children you are spirits. Try to think more of the spirit than the flesh, especially when preparing to work with spirit. In your quiet times of contemplation/meditation, let the flesh fall away. The more you let the flesh disperse then thoughts will go with it, leaving you free to concentrate on the connection with your own spirit and then the spirit peoples in our spheres. It would be beneficial if more worked in this way. We acknowledge the brain is hard to silence so we say, "Sleep brain and take my body with you as just for this short time I am my spirit self, which I wish to know more and connect with the true side of life. For I am a spirit above all things.

*****

A little more information will I impart as not all questioning can be answered or rather be permitted to be answered by us in the higher side of life. If all were revealed, then there would be little point in taking on the mantle of a body and of progression. The excitement of searching and knowing would be lost. The brain and mind revel in the inquisitive, explorations, discovering and solving enigmas. As you learn from birth the outer world around you, so as you mature you must learn the inner world of yourselves as spirits. The purpose of life in the body form is working towards attainment, knowledge, development of personality to synchronize with the unfolding spirit condition. The spiritual being has developed from the smallest forms of spirit through periods of consciousness in order to achieve its state of the higher ethical and spiritual abilities you know and see all around you today. Moral aspects of the spirit are sometimes lacking and wanting in some beings and therefore in the body condition, opportunity and experience are available to change and correct deficiencies. Whatever state is reached while in the body, all non-physical faculties survive are retained and is unaffected when the physical body is ceased.

Following the immediate change called death, the spirit is still clothed in matter and wears the clothing just prior to his or her passing, although lighter in texture as it adjusts to its surroundings and environment. This condition may last as long as it takes for the newly emerged spirit to accept its passing, acknowledge its surroundings and is ready to move forward away from the earth's conditioning and into the worlds of spirit. If their choice is to keep close to the earth plane in regarding to work or the welfare of loved ones still in the body, they will keep their dress in the fashion of their time and custom. However, at the point when a spirit has reached their level of evolvement they dispense with earthly fashions and adopt garments with textures relating to the place accredited them."

*****

Thought has direct action. The mind in spirit is always in the thinking mode and has more power in its true setting of the spirit worlds. When creation is needed, groups migrate together to plan, add in their expertise and a collective decision is made of the size, style and function of the construction. There is no laborious labour or arduous effort involved in the making. However, skills displayed when on the earth place, of craftsmanship are used in a likened manner to personalise the project and give pleasure to those wishing to display their talents and abilities. Unlike your dreams that are fragments and evaporate when attention is draw away, creation by mind in spirit has permanency, is fixed, sturdy and solid. Each creation fits to its surroundings and just as on earth has purpose, is used and appreciated. As the brain is dispensed with through transition, so the mind now governs. It is taught, it learns and gains knowledge just as the brain once did, but mind has expansion, has nothing to impede through poverty, class, age, disability. It is given freedom to express in all our known arts and more, freedom to create and engage in activities denied for some in the earth journey. Your true home therefore is not vapour or formless. View it as you would the earth in solid form. Growth and life still follows its natural sequence.

*****

Those on the earth who are able to give proof of the life beyond death, we know are often shunned, labelled with a mental imbalance, and it is said contacting spirits is the work of evil. Do they not realize that God is the supreme Spirit? Are they not aware that the spirits they speak of are the loved ones gone before them? They, who loved, nurtured and cared for you while on the earth have not suddenly changed into the wicked, have not changed their emotions only increased them, have no wish to hurt, give fear or harm and are far removed from spirits called devil. They are just the same as when on earth – righteous, protecting, honest beings. Words such as evil spirits have been passed down through ages of intolerance and ignorance. They have no place in the present time of free thinkers. The stemming of the soul growth is often caused by people who *preach* the words of God rather than prove the works of God. Many times we hear the words of a preacher and hear the sound of a child. For an undeveloped soul has much to learn of itself before it has right to preach to others.

*****

In times of upheaval and crisis the earth dwellers face, you are not abandoned. Evolution is never smooth but is necessary and part of the greater plan to grow and learn. It is at times of disruption gripping the earth that questioning, seeking answers and a period of learning begins. One sees the fragility of the body, the speed of transitions and fear grips. However, if acceptance of the spirit was not limited to a few, more would have of the capacity to accept their true selves, acquire a greater understanding of the responsibilities needed to evolve the soul and face and walk the pathway essential for improving the spirit within.

The expansion of the spirit through growth and development gives illumination which surrounds the spirit, presenting the appearance of a larger form in comparison to the human body. When power or stronger energy gained by a spirit through progression is spoken of, it is not to dominate or influence. The power is necessary to condition the spirit body in readiness for an elevated sphere that it has earned through advancement and to accept the more intense atmosphere that will prevail there. Never waste the gift of the earth time. As you progress through your experiences you are growing the spirit, although for most this is unseen by earthly vision. Expansion of your energy field encompasses the body, stands proud of your frame and is the beacon of a flourishing soul. Exercise of the body benefits the whole as is exercise of the mind. However, for the spirit to grow it is only a portion of these things. It is the human being you have made yourself in the circumstances around you, how you live in and through the experiences presented. Reaction to each situation gives opportunities no matter how small the response; a smile can brighten the face on both the giver and receiver as the energy flow connects giving the soul a little more growth through kindness. It is acts of thoughtfulness in the simplest forms for all of life, bonding the worlds together. We are not separate from spirit, can never be. Spirit is us – as we are spirit. Be confident in the greater plan for this small span of life in the body, it is just one grain of knowledge to be taken home and shared. You are an amazing being, a life-force before birth and after transition. You are what you will always be, a spirit with the sole purpose of growing itself.

*****

Sitter's question: "What is meant by pushing the energy through the vessel?"
Because of the many years of working with this vessel [medium] and the gradual build in development, those in spirit closest to her in the

working connection can now speak through the voice box extension with ease and fluency. We can enter her frame fusing energy to energy enabling expansion and movement of what you normally see is the solid human body. What we see is a gyrating, moving mass of molecules, atoms which when at transfer of the energy we set aside, separate and occupy the space created. The medium relinquishes control, her spirit steps aside into her energy field [aura] allowing occupancy for the short but allocated period during what is termed séance.

The stronger the energy force we inject into the vessel the more manipulation is conducted to accommodate the energy flow, without causing discord to the body or spirit. Opening points on the spirit body are transferred to the opening points on the flesh body, you call chakra. When these are activated, the stronger energy is pushed; energy in a more diluted form is passed through hands, feet, ears, face and more. When the energy has been successfully passed through, experiments can be undertaken in voice control, transfiguration, showing of spirit forms and much more depending on the medium's acceptance, conditioning and progression. The earth's energies do important and wondrous things, likewise spirit energy, but with added value. Each needs a source, a conductor to produce an effect; ours are mediums, without whom we would have a small spark instead of a flame.

*****

When you open the door to spirit at such times of séance, we take the opportunity to introduce those in spirit not yet accustomed to the methods of communicating in this manner. Minds in the fields of science are always present to analyse the work to try and overcome difficulties in communication methods or passing matter through matter. When returning to their allotted realms, work is continued, carried out in the areas of transmission not only for this period in the earth's evolution but for incarnations to come. We cannot afford to lose the link with the earth plane. We acknowledge technology often outstrips itself, so we too have to devise techniques to keep apace and improve methods or find other possibilities in contacting and interconnecting. We cannot apply everything in our world of living to the earth plane as we too are not privileged to know everything. We must find ways of using our minds to solve problems just as you do. Create methods of communicating so as to give proof of our presence and life, to offer reassurance of what waits beyond the body. If one chooses to search and listen, then we will reveal in the many ways possible. Many remain blind and deaf to the words of spirit but still we try to engage.

*****

It is wonderful to come and to speak on the voice box once more. It is a memory for some and a difficulty for others that will be learnt and overcome. In the spirit world our way of communication is mainly through mind. On certain levels the voice is still used constantly and especially at a time of adjustment following transition, but it is quickly dispensed with when trying to converse with many cultures newly arrived to spirit, and whose languages were not learnt or the opportunity was not given to learn, on the earth side of life. A training programme is offered, and more often than not, readily accepted and the skill of mind-to-mind communication is remembered, rekindled and becomes part of the adjustment back into the spirit self and into our natural world. There is always something to learn and the excitement of mastering and the eagerness for the next lesson in moving forward, is met with the willingness of being taught and in turn, teaching. When we speak to you in this way through the method of voice control, it is not a step back in progression, for using the voice box is a skill that has taken at length to learn and to hear the words in sounds connected to the earth's vibration once more, gives great pleasure and recollection of our own events when in the body state. Our world is not of silence, we have the dual method of mind or voice communication, and each has the preference. As our environment is fashioned to a less dense, weighted energy, words spoken have an altered tenor as our senses are heightened and the spirit form has many more senses than the body's five, which enable a wider scope in the methods of communicating. Shall we use the example of a drum and harp. Each one is heard with pleasure and meaning but the sound received on the senses is unmistakably altered.

One of the pleasures in the spirit world is when an opportunity is given to visit places where civilisations, styles of buildings or dress and mind processes, differ greatly from any understandings that you may have experienced. In these situations mind-to-mind communication breaks down barriers and offers a language to all.

Sitter's question – "Do you think in the future that when we are in the human state, mind-to-mind conversing would become the norm?"

This cannot be answered fully but if this is of help, we say, spirit is evolving and therefore anything and everything is possible and if it were in future plans then it would in some respect be an advantage, because there would be more understanding between persons, more tolerance and awareness of the inner self. But perhaps this would also open up a too easier pathway of progressing oneself spiritually. A large part of our progression is in communication with all spheres and overcoming the difficulties each layer of life brings. In the earth condition, instead of overcoming and accepting all people's predicaments with forbearance and compassion together with physical effort, mind-to-mind contact may take away in some degree, those things mentioned. Although you have technology to enhance and forward your lives and which has, and is, expanding greatly, it is not always technology that links you with the spirit worlds. Mind connection is a dissimilar knowledge, but there is always the possibility in the design of progression in adjusting or reworking the way communication is delivered. Direct spirit voice has been achieved and voice box communication mastered. So although mind communication is not deliverable yet on the earth from person to person, remember we who are presently in spirit, have dispensed with the brain and therefore use mind chiefly. Whereas in the body the mind is in partnership with the brain and because of this dual purpose to meet the earth conditions and to give the soul in its human condition the opportunity to further itself, dialogue for the foreseeable future is the main tool in development. Whether it is through tongue, hands or written word etcetera. In answer to the question we would say – hopefully and be hopeful and trust progression in all things."

"MAY THE LIGHT OF GOD THAT SHINES WITHIN ALL LIFE BE MADE BRIGHTER BY YOUR PROGRESSION"

INVITATION TO THE SÉANCE ROOM

This chapter has been left until the very end of the book purposely to give the reader a choice as to whether to read or not depending on their interest in séance activities.

So the reader, has some idea how the work is progressing with spirit, I give you an opportunity here to sit in on one of our séances. These small excerpts are from a sitting held in my home in 2018. Each sitting is recorded, at present via a digital recorder, then transferred to a memory stick and housed on a computer, adding to, and building up, a séance library. Over the years of working, tape recordings have given way to discs and now to digital recording and usb's. No doubt other methods of recording our sittings will appear as technology advances.

I hope you will excuse the informality of the text and try to visualise, a small group of ordinary people, meeting and speaking with spirit. The flow of conversation is natural between themselves and the spirit people. Sitter's names are not included (with the exception of our two guests who kindly consented) as I respect the privacy of those giving time to this work. Some of the regular sitters have family members who are not aware of their involvement in this work, also work colleagues and those they meet socially, to whom the revealing of their identities may cause awkwardness or embarrassment for those uneducated in spirit contact and communication methods. This I know may raise suspicion of the authenticity of what was seen and heard. The sittings were recorded, but even this, for some, will not give proof. The proof lies in actually being present in the séance room. However, I hope those of an open mind will accept what transpired and those searching for answers will gain a little insight into the happenings of our séance room. I have kept the spirit controllers input to just two named. However, throughout the sitting many more added their voices, faces, forms and expertise.

24/07/2018 – Séance lasted one hour forty-five minutes –the following small extracts may be of interest:

In the presence of Stephen Barrie (physical medium) and Christine Barrie of Holme Hall (Healing/Spiritual Centre) North Yorkshire UK

An opening prayer is given.

Spirit controllers – Little Raven on my left side, my maternal grandmother on the right side and White Eagle standing behind was acknowledged. The accustomed swelling sensation at the throat and surrounding area commenced followed by drowsiness.

Spirit Controller, Little Raven:
Raven blesses you, we work together, yes? And

come in peace and to the love that awaits us. I prepare the vessel for working, to control the vibration as the energy is introduced. Welcome friends old and new but all friends are 'long-standing to spirit'. Welcome brothers and sisters. Working with you is not work when we have joy. As the energy builds, there is the link from sphere to sphere and then we are here with you in the present, ourselves as much as is possible. For what is a voice without the love behind it? What is the personality without the heart that beats? We come to you in all manner possible to prove life of the spirit and with the continuity of life there is no barrier, no obstacle just movement, always movement, opportunities to push forward the work to progress and elevate. This communion between the worlds is not possible without the seed of love. It is the growth, the beginning, it is the whole. We need the vibration of joy for when there is mirth there is light within you. The light is seen, and felt, the light draws us closer to you. It is your light that attracts the spirit, the spirit within you and the spirit gathering around you. Everyone has the ability to work for spirit, singularly or collectively. You may say "But I am not a medium so therefore I cannot work spiritually." But this is incorrect because you are a spirit and therefore everything is possible, and although you may not be on the ability level to draw in spirit or see spirit, there is no reason or barrier preventing you from the practices of spirit work because you are a spirit and therefore it is your right to try. You are born with the ability to communicate to all life forms. Acceptance of spirit within and before you, indicates a mind expanding and a heart that is full of love

White Eagle:
"We commence the work process with your permission and begin with instruction from time to time for dark and red-light conditions."

Comments from the sitters – in dim red light:
"Spirits are walking around in front of us the table is moving and raising up."

In full red light (illuminating all of the medium) – Stephen and Christine (Barrie) speaking:
There is something draped over the medium's face and behind it looks skeletal. It's gone darker now and there is a face building now with rather a large nose. Sparkling lights around the throat area. There are lines on the medium's face now and many changes with and an Indian's face appearing. I know this energy level its familiar to me. The face is changing into an old man's, an old Indians face, I can see his teeth. There is something on the head in black coming down the forehead. There is a lady now with a beehive hairstyle like they had in the 1960, a smile and a strong pair of eyes. There is another Indian now much younger with pigtails at either side of the head. An African face, and there is illumination around the neck and chest area. Look at the

medium's body now it's expanding, the arms, shoulders are all increasing in size. This is a much larger person than the medium. There is my Mum appearing – I can see you Mum, Yes, Yes so can I, look there is a smile, I can see her eyes, she is looking to the side. Hello Mum, look she is pretending to put her lipstick on. She did like her make-up and she is waving just like she did, blowing kisses and blowing one back to you Mum, oh we love you too. I can see her face so clear now, yes well-done Mum. She is still there, still hanging on. She hasn't come through anyone before. I have had one clairvoyant message from her but nothing like this. My Mum would only come through certain people and the medium is one! It's the medium's type and character that would attract her. There is an extreme amount of energy – none of this is normal at all. We are very privileged. There are only a few mediums like this one, who could do this.

There is so much energy surrounding the medium's head. Its illumination and there is light passing from one hand to another, it's coming out from her hands. The right hand is brighter, white and bluish light coming from it. There are loads going on now. The energy is building into quite a mass. As the light moves it is leaving a trail of light behind it. There is someone [spirit] moving behind her, look the face is changing, disappearing and coming back, spirit are walking around again, working. The energy is shooting up another foot higher than normal with the mass of energy. There are more spirit people behind her now and it looks like the walls have disappeared to accommodate them, the space has got bigger. It has all gone completely black now, no light seen at all. It's coming back now and a large swirl of energy going up towards the ceiling. There is a head and a face appearing on the medium's torso. There is also a little face in the energy as she is holding her hand up. It's constant and fascinating.

Philosophy from Controller White Eagle:

We are here with you, and we welcome. Now my friends what can we achieve at this time? We can achieve the vibration that elevates; lifting hearts and minds so that it is easy for spirit to come to work and to be with you. In the first contacts with spirit it is not all about work, it is about the presence, the knowing, and the accepting and then we consider the work. Nothing is to be rushed for in rushing you miss things: steady pace, you see things. We prefer the steadiness, the stability of the mind, the body and the thinking process. We wish to help in many ways, but it is not all concerning the proof, it is the feel of the spirit within, the energy that awakens that spirit and plants the seed in the mind of wishing to know more. Questions such as "I wish to know what is beyond the body when transition occurs." It is also controlling the sub-consciousness we have the subconscious on the lower levels. Yes, there is personality there which can interfere with the work, so we try to help with control, but this must be done chiefly by self, not spirit! Self must develop the techniques of controlling the sub-consciousness and then allowing the energy and personality of the spirit-being to draw close in readiness to work with the higher consciousness. Words come easy but the work is difficult as we cannot make your pathway easy. We aid, encourage and move you along but not without the willingness of self. One light, one love, we are family with one purpose to work, advance and grow. The connections you make on the soul's journey are not by chance but by design. Even the ones that give difficulty, doubts, fear, and uncertainty as these are building the character within. There are so many facets to this work because while we are working with you other activities are being carried out. When creating a link with the earth-plane we are able to enhance work in our worlds too. When you come to spirit it will become clearer as to why you have made certain connections during your human life. In spirit you are clothed in your progression, and this is the light you give out and other spirits who in turn become inspired by your light and so wish to emulate.

No doubt my friends you have heard the collective term of soul grouping. This is a very complex issue. It sounds simplicity itself, but it is not. The soul group can consist of very few, they are in the hub of gathering more and some can be humongous in number. The purpose of these large groups is to reach, not only the earth-plane and its many directions, but outwards to other spheres. If you are not of accepting what I portray I will still continue to speak, for one day you will (I ask forgiveness for I do not mean to undermine your intelligence at this stage but in our learning, it is a continuity to learn for this is expansion of the mind and of the spirit). Within these soul groups lies a nucleus, it is the beating heart of the energy. The souls closer to this nucleus are the stronger highly evolved. Those souls on the extremities receive less of the energy as they cannot receive more at this stage of development, but they are non-the-less important to the work. From time to time a member from the nucleus will reach out, materialise and take the body form and come to the earth-plane so those in the extremities can gain knowledge, have the connection to the earth-plane and benefit. The one on the earth plane is placed there to expand the knowledge, for there is always something, shall we say a little different in the make-up of this being for they have come for a purpose not just for the earth-plane but for the soul group that they have connection with. They are a steppingstone and when they return to the spirit and the nucleus, others will take their place on the earth-plane for it is a continuity of knowledge, expansion and stronger energy.

We are aware that some do not accept incarnation, it is abhorrent to them, for in the body state there is limitation for acceptance, but it is a course that is natural within the law of nature and spirit growth and when you are of an acceptance of this it plays a huge part in the growth of the soul group. To incarnate to the earth-plane or other spheres is a joy with all the tribulations of hardship, pain, grief it is still a joy for your soul is growing. It is also of giving to the soul group you have left – it is a finite gift. So all the experience goes back to the soul group – it is not just for yourself for you are part of a link. Yes, you gain on a personal level but your connection, your higher purpose; your super consciousness is connected to the group what is growing, vibrating, pulsating, shedding the light and also growing closer to the light that you are contributing much to. There is creation it has been said and I again echo the words, creation is being created, it is ongoing for there is no ceasing to expansion. Embrace all that you receive, I know there are contradictions in accepting incarnate for you ask one spirit friend "do we have re-birth?" they answer "Oh no no no," you ask another and they say "Oh yes yes yes." The soul that says 'no no no' is only giving his or her view of the place and the stage they are in, they cannot view further for they have not progressed and cannot see the end of their pathway. While they are developing, they can only be given what they can accept in their level of living. So when you have the negative of a no, do not take this as truth. Think for yourselves, always expand the mind and do not have any limitations for if you have limitations of your mind, you limit yourself in growth. You are not fools and you do analyse but when you analyse try to be visionary.

Sitters:
Thank you White Eagle.

Sitters speaking – in full red light, directed at the medium:
This face over the medium's is staying longer, not just fleeting as the others did; they are staying and wanting to be seen. It is a gentleman with very dark eyes, a defined chin and jawline. Very handsome face. It is so intriguing. On the left side there is a dense mass of energy not attached to the medium. The base of the neck has puffed up again and there is something coming out, it is light in colour. There is someone smiling, oh definitely it's a man and there is another face showing, not a child's face but a very young face. The energy surrounding is constantly moving; it is certainly interesting to watch. We are actually now seeing spirit shapes and forms, amazing.

Spirit controller:
We try to keep the work to a certain level in the spectrum of the rays that the red light affords, if too little light we are unseen, too much we are unseen. We need the balance to give the effect more pronounced prominence. We hope that this has been achieved and your vision has captured the energy that is of spirit. Thank you most graciously for participating in our time together.

Sitters:
We thank you very much.

Spirit controller Little Raven:
> We are mindful of the limitations of energy, but we know that we will return soon. We take our leave, we take your love and we leave you our love. To be remembered is wonderful. By name, face and beating heart is wonderful. We never forget you.
>
> A closing prayer is given.

The séance work continues to the present day. With spirit bringing in more of the denser energy that engulfs the whole of my body, emanating from the solar plexus, cascading down to floor level before rising up to become spirit forms, allowing their movement around the séance room. Together with transfiguration and the expansion of the voice-box mechanism it is a remarkable achievement of spirit and so much more to experience and look forward to.

Never be content to stay at the same level of ability when working with spirit, there is so much more to gain by propelling yourself further in the field of mediumship.

CONCLUSION

Reader, it is time to conclude. There is only so much that I can divulge on the subject of spirit, energy or mediumship without over burdening or causing boredom. I have related my journeying through spirit education given so far. I acknowledge the small amount that I am imparting but this field of learning has an enormity and my lessons have been brief, having had to fit in with material settings and episodes of parenting, career and general life.

As spirits we belong to the Universal Spirit, we are not supernatural as this would set us in the abnormal. To be a spirit therefore is to be normal. To converse with other spirits is normal. To transition from body to spirit is normal. We have taken on the human form in order to learn who we are and what we will become, through experiences encountered and gained, all in the normal processes of human life.

I therefore draw the curtain dividing the material and the spirit worlds and invite you from time to time to open the drapes on your spirit self and the pathway of your choice. You will not be disappointed, you will never reach the end of learning but the advantages of discovery and partaking are Energies of and for the Soul and outweigh any material benefits.

Be Human   Be Self   Above all,   Be Spirit

www.ingramcontent.com/pod-product-compliance
Lightning Source LLC
LaVergne TN
LVHW041635060526
838200LV00040B/1580